In the Shadow of a Legend
DILIP KUMAR

In the Shadow of a Legend DILIP KUMAR

Faisal Farooqui

Om Books International

First published in 2022 by

Om Books International

Corporate & Editorial Office
A-12, Sector 64, Noida 201 301
Uttar Pradesh, India
Phone: +91 120 477 4100
Email: editorial@ombooks.com
Website: www.ombooksinternational.com

Sales Office
107, Ansari Road, Darya Ganj,
New Delhi 110 002, India
Phone: +91 11 4000 9000
Fax: +91 11 2327 8091
Email: sales@ombooks.com
Website: www.ombooks.com

ISBN: 978-93-92834-66-0

Printed in India

10 9 8 7 6 5 4 3 2 1

For Saira Baji

Contents

Acknowledgements

The book you are holding in your hands is a part of my life, a journey undertaken with the legendary Dilip Kumar. When I first met him, I was a ten-year-old schoolboy and he, already one of the world's leading stars.

You know him as an exceptional actor, but I want you to see him through my eyes. The conversations I've had, my interactions with him, words shared over casual evening teas, car rides and sunset walks, or late-evening silent reflections at Jogger's Park. The twenty years post-college I've looked up to him have been among the most enriching moments in my life.

I always seemed to be asking him the most difficult questions, without realizing that I was perhaps at times making him uncomfortable. I've contemplated this with my brother, Asif, and my wife, Aabeda, numerous times. She usually laughed and teased me that it's probably because he thought of me as a son.

Although this book is about my journey with Dilip Sahab, it would not have been possible without the impeccable guidance and help of some very fine people in my life.

I would like to begin by thanking my mother. Her prayers and hard work are the reason I have the intellect and strength to write this book. Her unfortunate demise during the course of writing this book only strengthened my resolve to finish it. Amma's life is an inspiration to me.

Asif Farooqui, my brother, without you this book would have never happened. Why you felt the need to introduce me to Dilip Sahab is something I will never be able to figure out. If it wasn't for you, I would never have had the opportunity to learn the intricacies of life from the ever-insightful Dilip Kumar.

No story about Dilip Sahab's life is complete without the woman who has stood by him throughout these years. Saira Baji, no words are enough to convey how thankful I am for all the stories and anecdotes you shared over the years about your life with Sahab. The love with which you describe your time with him will always have a special place in my heart. I am forever amazed at your infatuation with Dilip Sahab, and the dedication you have displayed as a wife and companion.

Udaya Tara Nayar, the one person outside the family who knew Dilip Sahab as well as he knew himself. Our conversations helped me understand Dilip Sahab better than I could ever have imagined. Your quiet hints and explanations gave me the opportunity to finish the manuscript faster than I had anticipated. I will always be thankful to you for this.

My brothers – Shuaib, Asif, Javed, Suhail and Hamid – and sisters – Shaheda, Masooda, Ishrat and Nishat – I would like to thank you for taking care of me, your youngest sibling, and guiding me to be the man I am today. Your love and support gave me the platform to be an entrepreneur, and now, maybe a writer.

Aabeda, my lovely wife, thank you for being my constant support. You have stood by me at all times, carried our life and our children, and have been the pillar I lean on. My strength comes from you.

My charming bhabhis, my beautiful children – Shiraz, Kashif, Basit, Haifa – and my wonderful nieces and nephews, all of whom I have bored for hours talking about my adoration for Dilip Kumar over dinners, long drives and family vacations. Thank you for listening patiently.

Dr Jalil Parkar, Sahab's friend and chest-specialist, grateful for your invaluable support in sickness and in health.

Zaitun Khan, my personal assistant, a sincere thank you for your administrative support. Soma Das for your generous advice and guidance at every stage. Aftab Siddiqui for proofreading the Urdu inputs and Maria Sarfaraz for your invaluable help in fixing the conversation of a profound, life-changing event which Sahab had narrated to me in Hindko dialect. You'll find this in Chapter 7.

I must acknowledge that the manuscript would not have been possible without the wholehearted dedication of my special assistant Shalki Khanna. My admiration and gratitude for Kanishka Gupta, my friend and literary agent, whose tireless effort made this book a reality along with the publisher, Shantanu Ray Chaudhuri.

To my readers, thank you for picking up this book. I hope you enjoy reading it as much as I have enjoyed living and writing it.

Author's Note

We are from God and to Him we return.

I finished writing this book in June 2019. Some of the dearest people who've been mentioned in this book have since left for the hereafter: Amma (my mother) on 9 June 2019, Ahsan Bhai (Dilip Kumar Sahab's brother) in August 2020, Aslam Bhai (Dilip Kumar Sahab's brother) in September 2020, and Sahab on 7 July 2021. I feel they are all still with me, with those of us who loved them and were fortunate to know them.

The decision to write this book was not an easy one. Dilip Kumar, Dilip Sahab or simply Sahab, as all of us would address him, narrated an autobiographical account between 2004 and 2006. After that he stopped dictating and the manuscript which Udaya Tara Nayar completed was put on hold. Finally, the task of finalizing a publisher was assigned to me and in June 2014, the autobiography was released.

Friends and family complained that there was so much to Dilip Kumar than what was written in the autobiography. That is true, I realized. Dilip Kumar was an ocean and any number of books will not be enough to know his complete personality. Sahab was a man of few words. In all honesty he was not too keen to publish his own life-story. He was a shy man. So, in

2016, I decided that I'd write a book on my hero, Dilip Kumar, as the person I have come to know. Not as a popular actor or celebrity, but as a friend, maybe even a father figure.

The challenge was that my years of closeness with Dilip Sahab were never recorded on tape or diary – I never felt the need for it. It was everyday life. In the mid-1990s, as a student, I had impressed many US college admission officers and professors with my powerful memory. It's a boon and a bane. So when I sat down to write this book I could still feel Dilip Sahab holding my hand. I could still experience the fragrance of the warm winds while we spoke. I could recall everything. I could recall the way he sat and expressed a certain incident or story to me. The journey to Mecca with Dilip Sahab was so vivid, everything just so fresh in my mind. And so, I began to write.

Through informal conversations and witty exchanges, I have tried to capture the private side of the man the world worships. I've tried to portray his love for others, his childhood, his stubborn nature and his need to do good for the underprivileged. Perhaps you will find the stories as enticing and educational as I did. While on one side you get lost in the lanes of Peshawar, on the other, you learn life lessons from the homilies he shared, on how to succeed in life, and how to deal with failure, among so many other lessons. I want to thank the legend for unknowingly teaching me about living in his shadow.

Faisal Farooqui
Mumbai, February 2022

1

'Milte Rehna':
The First Time I Met Sahab

The Second World War had just got over. British India split into India and Pakistan. People lost their lives, families their homes, and countless their livelihood. A cloud of woe loomed all over. From this anguish emerged a man – a romantic, brightening the gloomy skies, the ray of sunshine that India needed. He was a hero, on screen and off it.

It has often been said that there were only two types of people post-1947: those who knew Dilip Kumar and his movies, and those who were obsessed with Dilip Kumar and his movies. I belong to a category which was not yet defined – those who knew almost nothing of his movies, but know Muhammad Yusuf Khan. His screen name Dilip Kumar resonated every time it was uttered in any room. The world knew the actor who took on the might of Emperor Akbar for his lady love. They knew him as the romantic hero who stole hearts. I, though, knew him as a person. Not a legend, not a superstar, but a person.

I consider myself lucky to have known him as more than the actor that he was. I've never had any special interest in movies or Indian cinema, but that bustling winter afternoon of 1987 is still fresh in my mind. It was a Thursday. My school had its weekly off and I was looking forward to a day of pointless games fuelled by my puerile imagination. Instead, I was asked to get dressed to greet an esteemed guest. There was a huge hustle-bustle all around the house. My mother, brothers, bhabhi, sisters – everyone was scurrying about, fixing food, themselves and the house.

My sister's words from that afternoon still echo in my mind, *"Jaldi karo! Dilip Sahab khaane pe ghar aa rahe hain!"* (Quick! Dilip Sir is coming home for a meal!).

I cannot forget how berserk every member in my family went the first time Sahab came home. It's my first memory of him.

A tall man. An assuring presence, well built. It wasn't just his physical appearance but his demeanour that commanded respect. He seemed to overpower everything in our humble home. Every word he spoke was soft, yet commanding. Everyone in my family was enraptured. I stared at the magnificent creature sitting on our beautiful sofa. I crouched behind my elder siblings, allowing the man to speak with them. He spoke with me briefly once. Asked me about my school, and then the adults resumed their conversation.

Since then, my awareness and admiration of Dilip Kumar or Sahab has only grown.

Our family first knew of him through one of my elder brothers, Asif Bhai. He was introduced to Sahab when he was a fresher in college.

Dilip Sahab obviously encountered dozens of people almost every day, but he had a way of reading them. It was as if he was looking through them, right into their soul, and recognizing them as the person and talent that they were, not what they portrayed in front of him.

He had once been invited to grace an event as the chief guest. This was for a play put up by a troupe of college students at Darjeeling. Sahab would attend as many invitations as he could from the dozens of requests he received every month. I think it was his second nature to be among people and interact with them. There was a sense of intrigue in his interaction with others. Always knowledgeable and curious, Sahab was perceptive enough to identify a diamond in the rough, and he never shied away from appreciating people's hard work and efforts.

He really enjoyed the play put up by the amateur performers. He wanted to meet the professor who had written and directed it. The humble educator stepped out in front of him, shoulders slouched, hands joined together, and happiness in his eyes. Sahab asked him, "What do you teach?"

"Sir, I'm a professor of engineering. I enjoy writing stories. And drama too. So, I have worked on this play with the students."

Sahab placed a hand of encouragement on the professor's shoulder and said, "*Bohot khoobsurti se aapne apni mehnat samney layi hai. Milte rehna.*" (You've presented your hard work beautifully. Stay in touch.)

The humble professor's voice quivered as he graciously bowed and thanked Dilip Kumar. He stayed in touch, and just recently, we bade him goodbye on his unfortunate demise. That humble college professor was Kader Khan.

*

Johnny Walker was another great personality Dilip Sahab discovered. Contrary to how superstars were expected to behave, Dilip Sahab often took Bombay's famed trams and buses in his younger days. Anyone who has been to Bombay understands how crowded these buses can get. Even the smallest man would have a hard time finding a seat. Fortunately for one conductor, Sahab didn't bother about these trivial issues. Dilip Sahab saw him walk from one end of the bus to the other, announcing in a typical nasal voice, "Ticket! Ticket! Ticket! Ticket!"

The man intrigued Sahab, and he couldn't stop admiring his unique style of walking. He called out to him for a brief chat.

"*Milte rehna*," he said to the humble bus conductor after talking to him. He would go on to introduce him to Bimal Roy. And another legend, Johnny Walker, was born.

Milte rehna.

A simple statement that changed many lives.

*

He had said the same golden words to Asif Bhai, and those words have given me the opportunity to discover so many insights on life and about Sahab. My brother told me how he met him for the first time at Sahab's home. Asif Bhai was a young college boy at the time. After being introduced to Dilip Sahab through a mutual friend, Asif Bhai decided to visit his home at Pali Hill, which was just a few blocks away from our house. It was a huge house, teeming with people. It was never easy walking into it without a prior appointment.

But here was my brother, innocent of the ways of celebrity homes, brave, determined, and completely mesmerized by the golden words, *milte rehna*.

One afternoon, he got ready in his finest clothes and marched up to Sahab's house. He managed to convince the watchmen and went up to Sahab's office across the hall, his mind soaking in its beauty. Suddenly a man grabbed his arm from behind. He seemed to be much older but his grip was firm and his voice was stern. He asked Asif Bhai, "Where do you think you're going?"

With audacious confidence, my brother responded, "I want to meet Dilip Kumar."

The man, his voice booming, said, "Everyone here wants to meet Dilip Kumar. Who are you?"

Unfazed, Asif Bhai added some timbre to his own voice. "Who are you?"

"I am Ahsan. Dilip Kumar is my brother." His eyes pierced through my brother.

Asif Bhai told me that in that moment he couldn't feel his legs anymore. It was as if someone had pulled the ground from right under him. He had spoken rudely to Dilip Kumar's brother.

Soon after, Dilip Sahab became close to Asif Bhai and through him to our family. My brother fondly remembers that day even today, and talks about it to anyone willing to lend him an ear. Over the years, Sahab's family, and even his extended family, became close to the Farooqui family. And Ahsan Khan, with his baritone, became a great family friend – not just Dilip Kumar's brother. Saira Banu, who doesn't need any introduction, once said to us, "Faisal and Asif, you are like my children."

One of my earliest profound memories with Sahab was when my eldest brother was about to reach a prominent milestone in life. Shuaib Bhai had spent years training to be a doctor, a paediatric surgeon. In the late 1980s, after finishing his residency, he moved to Saudi Arabia to begin his practice. A year later, when he returned on a holiday, he met Dilip Sahab over a cup of tea.

My brother fondly recalled to me his conversation with Dilip Sahab.

"That man has inspired me in ways I cannot explain. I was happy in Saudi. I was earning more than I could ask for. When

Dilip Sahab spoke to me, the only thing he said was, why don't you come back and serve your country. The way he said it, his intensity, I just had to come back."

The year was 1990. Shuaib Bhai, having paid heed to Sahab's advice, was now starting his clinic-cum-office in Bombay. He had extended an invitation to Dilip Sahab, requesting his presence as chief guest to inaugurate the clinic.

As Sahab cut the ribbon and entered the blue-and-white room, he looked at the people gathered. With a calm but proud smile, he made a short speech. I still remember his words, "*Ek aur bachcha hamara aaj parbaan chadha.*"

I didn't understand what he meant, as I had not yet been exposed to chaste Urdu. I later discovered that the expression 'parbaan chadhna' meant achieving fulfilment.

Sahab had regarded my eldest brother as his own. With this statement, he expressed his pride at my brother's achievement, and prayed for his success.

Another memory of Dilip Sahab is at Asif Bhai's wedding in 1991. My brother was young, hard-working, and eager to start his life's next phase. I remember how happy he looked that day. Expectedly, he had invited Sahab. However, inviting someone like Dilip Kumar to a wedding is one matter. Having him turn up is another. After all, he was Dilip Kumar! But he took us by surprise.

The nikah was scheduled for 7 p.m. The whole house was bustling, and everyone was hurriedly getting ready. At 5.30 p.m., Asif Bhai went to his room to shower and get dressed. Around the same time, there was a hubbub outside the house. And there he was, Dilip Sahab, dressed to the nines, gracefully stepping out of his car, surrounded by a swarm of people. As he reached our house's main entrance, he turned around and addressed his entourage, "*Aap sab yahin rukiye. Main akele andar ja raha hoon. Yeh mere ghar waale hain.*" (I request you all to please wait here. I will go alone inside. They are my family.)

He proceeded to walk in with just one man in tow, probably a relative. He breezed up the stairs and enquired about Asif Bhai's whereabouts. I greeted him at the stairs with the rest of my family, and we guided him to the groom's chamber. My brother had just stepped out of the shower. A hundred purdahs would not have been able to hide the shock on his face.

Sahab announced with a smile, "*Main dulhe ko taiyyar karunga.*" (I will get the groom ready.)

In our culture, only the closest to the groom or bride enter their room and help them get ready. It is a privilege enjoyed only by close family and friends. Others are neither invited, nor do they try to come in.

But Sahab walked in. And in that moment, he was more than just a friend. He was family. To my brother, he was now somewhat of a father figure. I don't believe I had ever seen him happier.

*

Years later, I found out that Sahab had an important meeting to attend the very evening of my brother's nikah. Instead of cancelling or postponing either, he made an adjustment to his own schedule. He went above and beyond what was required of him. He could have skipped our invitation, given the importance of his meeting, but by showing up at our home, he made my brother's nikah that much more memorable and beautiful.

Through the years, with every interaction I have had with Dilip Sahab, I got closer to him. I felt like he was my own. It was as if I was speaking to a long-lost friend, or maybe a father figure in whom I found a guide. He didn't do it knowingly.

His words did the work for him, and sometimes his silence did. He never told me how to behave, or how to carry myself. He never spoke to me in a manner that would suggest that he wanted to influence me. Yet, his persona and presence made a huge impact on how I live my life today, both personally and professionally. His dedication to his work, the respect he gave every relationship in his life, and the simple, yet classy way in which he lived, all spoke volumes to me.

His words have played a subtle role in shaping me into the man I am today. His slight nudges, wise words, and his caring nature, all came together as he became a friend that I not just wanted but needed. He became a mentor to me. I watched him interact with the world, talk about his work, and have been a witness to some of his labour for the less privileged.

If I had to define him in one word, I would call him 'human'. For the world, he was an icon, a legend, and to some even a god. Sure, he was an actor whose work was defined by immersing himself in the character he played, an actor whose emotional bond with his close-knit family and subtle observations of childhood lingered in his heart till his last day, an actor who was a benchmark for all actors after him. However, in my eyes, he was a human being. A simple, yet, complicated human being. One who didn't have any miraculous powers, yet cast his spell on everyone who came in touch with him.

2

Parallel Lives

According to my mother, I had always been a happy but reserved child. Like Dilip Sahab's, we were a large family – ten brothers and sisters. Being the youngest in my family, I was shielded from the crisis that befell us when I was merely a few years old.

It was late 1981. As a young boy who had just started formal schooling, I recall the day my father and mother packed their bags to leave for our ancestral home town, Azamgarh, in Uttar Pradesh, for a 'few weeks'. The memories are vague, but I remember I was inconsolable. They were leaving me behind in Bombay to enjoy their trip, or so I thought as a young child angry at his parents for abandoning him.

As I had just been enrolled in school, my father thought it would be wise if I stayed back instead of accompanying them on a short trip. After all, it wouldn't look good if I went on leave so soon after my schooling started.

I clung to my father as they got ready to leave. He chuckled and turned around to hug me. "We will be back in a few days," he consoled me.

I wiped my tears and put on the brave big-boy face to bid my parents goodbye. My brothers and sisters were going to take care of me for the next few weeks. I would stay back, attend school, and wait till they came back, bringing with them bags filled with sweets, savouries, and perhaps even toys.

Next day, still upset by my parents' decision to leave, I returned to my boring school schedule. That night, in a quiet house, our phone rang. The loud ring coming from the instrument was incongruous against the dull streetlight throwing patterns on the walls of the large living room on the first floor of 48 Pali Village. It woke up a lot of us. It was a trunk call.

Back in the 1980s, a trunk call was the only way to reach someone long distance. To speak to someone residing in another town, one would have to dial the telephone department's trunk-booking number and book a trunk call with an operator. You would have to provide the details of the person you wished to speak to, their number in that city, and mention if you would like to book it as ordinary or urgent. The operator would then call you back when he could connect the number, request you to hold, attempt to call the other person, inform them of the call, and then finally connect. It was a long process, and often there would be some time gap between booking and actually getting the connection.

It was almost midnight when we received the call. My eldest sister's room was the closest to the main hall where the telephone was kept in our two-storeyed bungalow. Her husband, my brother-in-law, rushed to pick up the receiver, trying not to disturb anyone, especially the children, but I was already awake. The noise had startled me out of my peaceful slumber. I walked slowly across the living room and settled myself on the sofa, keenly watching my brother-in-law through sleep-heavy eyes. He spoke with the caller in a gruff voice, stifling yawns. As moments passed, his stance became stiffer, eyes wider, and his voice lost all traces of sleep. He mumbled something in a hushed, urgent tone, placed the receiver on the side, and ran towards the stairs. His heavy steps shook the floor as he glided downstairs. In a blink of an eye he was back at the phone. Shuaib Bhai was now with him. Half panting, my brother began speaking into the mouthpiece of the Bakelite receiver.

Slowly the entire house woke up. Lights were switched on in almost every room. There were no more dancing shadows on the walls. Just bright rooms, and darkness outside. Eager adults circled around the phone, waiting for the eldest man in the family to give them some answers. The atmosphere was tense. Slowly, as if all his energy had been drained, my brother kept the phone down to turn to the rest of the family. There was sad news – my father had passed away a few hours earlier.

I don't remember much, and I'm not sure if someone told me about what had happened, but the commotion and the wailing are clear in my mind even today. It scared me, watching the men and women raise their hands in prayer, crying uncontrollably. They embraced each other tearfully, adding to the anguish. I tried to sink into the sofa, hoping to disappear. I didn't know what had happened, and my scared heart didn't want to know anything at all.

Everyone was devastated, in deep shock. To imagine something like this was next to impossible. My father was the eldest of his siblings, patriarch of the extended Farooqui family, but still very young. In his prime, and healthy, his sudden demise was something no one was ready for. No one could possibly fathom why God had taken him away from us. I, being one of the younger ones, was not made privy to the details of what exactly happened.

*

Five long years after the ringing telephone had shattered the peace of the night I gathered the courage to ask my mother. She told me that my father had complained of chest pain in the train. He tried to put up a brave face, hoping the pain would pass. When he finally voiced his extreme discomfort, they were only a few hours away from home. My mother, being alone, didn't know what to do. From the railway station they drove home as fast as they could in a taxi. No sooner had they reached home, she rushed to get a glass of water for my father. When she came back from the kitchen, he had passed away in his chair in the verandah. Before they could even inform my uncle, a doctor.

I sympathized with my mother. It wouldn't have been easy for her to watch her husband writhe in pain and be unable to do anything. I cannot imagine how powerless she must have felt. The man she had married at the age of sixteen, and with whom she spent thirty-three years and raised ten children, had suddenly gone, and she couldn't do anything about it. It took her almost two years to get out of the grief-stricken phase. I don't think she ever recovered from the anguish of losing her companion. My mother passed away as I was completing this manuscript, in June 2019, thirty-eight years after my father.

For two years after my father's death, my eldest sister Shaheda Aapa took care of me and the younger siblings. She was in her late twenties, married, with kids of her own. She treated me and cared for me as if I was her son. She took care of me in the best way she could. She would dress me up for school and pack my lunch. For all purposes, for those long two years Shaheda Aapa was my mother. I will always have a special place for her in my heart.

Along with Shaheda Aapa, my other siblings also took on parental responsibilities. The second eldest sister, Masooda Aapa, was married and lived in a different town. She would call often and be there for us whenever she could. My eldest brother, Shuaib Bhaijan, became the man of the house. He was newly-wed, and had just finished medical school. Despite being occupied with his medical internship, he made sure that the household ran smoothly. He tried to fill in the vacuum our father had left behind. Earning, feeding, educating, my brother did it all. Asif Bhai, all of seventeen years himself, assisted Shuaib Bhai and managed the family's bakery business while still in college. They raised us, while leaning on each other for emotional and financial support.

The rest of us – Ishrat Aapa, Javed Bhai, Suhail Bhai, Nishat Aapa, Hamid Bhai and I – were all kids who turned into adults overnight. Closer in age, we became dependent on each other emotionally. We had just lost our father, and in so many ways for a brief period, our mother too.

*

Three years after my father's passing, Asif Bhai met Dilip Sahab for the first time. That's when Sahab came into our lives. Young as I was when my father passed away, I find it difficult to recollect his voice, but when I spoke with Dilip Sahab, I could imagine my father speaking in a similar manner. Wise, careful with his words, loving, and respectful. Maybe that's why Asif Bhai formed such a strong bond with the legendary actor.

When Dilip Sahab told me about the role Sakina Aapa (his oldest sister) played in their household, it reminded me of my sister and eldest brother. Sahab would often describe the loving and nurturing ways of Sakina Aapa, and how she was a mother to them. And I couldn't help reflect on my older brother and sister. I have seen a lot of similarities between Sahab's family and mine. Maybe that's why we remained close all through.

When Asif Bhai met Dilip Sahab, there was a connect. It was evident from both ends. Asif Bhai was a young man who had just lost his father. Dilip Sahab's love, care and guidance automatically made my brother see him as the father figure he had just lost. He would often ask Asif Bhai for his opinions on matters of work, and even personal decisions. Dilip Sahab became a part of our family, and we, his. Asif Bhai deserves more credit than anybody for building this bond with Dilip Sahab.

Sahab attended the weddings of almost all my siblings. Almost every member of my immediate family has been graced by his presence at important milestones in their lives. Surprisingly enough, Sahab was unable to attend my wedding. When I got married, Dilip Sahab was travelling for work. He did make sure that Naseem Banu and Saira Baji would be present at my wedding. They walked up to me to the wedding stage and confessed that Dilip Sahab had instructed them to make sure that I don't feel his absence at the event. It was a big deal considering Naseem Banu did not usually like stepping out. Of course, I missed Sahab's presence at my wedding, but I knew his blessings were always with me.

I'll probably never know why my bond with Sahab was so strong. I always seemed to be asking him the most difficult questions, without realizing that I was probably making him uncomfortable. I've contemplated this with my brothers and my wife, Aabeda, numerous times. She usually laughed and told me it's probably because he thought of me as a son. And this was clear from the most inconsequential of our interactions.

In 2001, the most popular movie of the year, *Dil Chahta Hai*, had released. It took the country by storm. Aamir Khan's 'cute' goatee and short spiked hair was all anyone could talk about. Like every other young man my age, I decided to grow a small goatee. I loved it. I was kicked and excited about it.

Needless to say, my wife hated it. For weeks on end, she would tell me how much she hated it, and couldn't wait for me to shave it off. I didn't budge.

All those days that I sported the goatee, Dilip Sahab would just look at me strangely. He once asked me about it, and, in a bashful manner, I told him that it was the 'latest fad'. I was a part of the 'it' crowd now. Then one day, when I was visiting him, he finally revealed to me his feelings about the goatee.

All afternoon, I had sat across from him, happily engrossed in conversation, absentmindedly playing with the stubble below my lip. After a while, I stood up to take his leave. I walked up to him, and as I bent over to hug him goodbye, he grabbed the small triangle-shaped lock of hair perched snugly under my lower lip. He yanked at it and asked me, "*Yeh kya hai?*" (What is this?)

With my goatee still clenched between his fingers, I replied meekly, flinching in pain, "*Sahab, yeh goatee aiwein hi maine rakhi hai. Aamir Khan ne rakhi thi Dil Chahta Hai movie mein.*" (Sahab, I've kept this goatee just like that. Aamir Khan had it in his film *Dil Chahta Hai*.)

"Why?"

"Everyone's sporting it. So, I thought even I'll."

He let go of my goatee. With a stern expression that made me shiver, he pointed one finger at me and instructed me to shave it off.

"*Shave karo isay. Bilkul saaf chehra hona chahiye.*" (Shave it. I want a clean face.)

I looked at Sahab and realized that he always had a clean face. Behind the cameras, he sported the same classic look. He never had an unruly mop or wore crazy clothes. He kept it simple and classic.

I succumbed. Nursing my bruised chin and ego, I left his home. Like a father screaming at his kids for getting involved with something new every day, Sahab had yelled at me. The scared child in me shaved it the next day. Even today, I keep my face clean.

My eldest son had his first encounter with a razor when he was in high school. It was a big day for both of us. As I taught him how to use the sharp blade, I realized I said the same thing to him that Dilip Sahab had said to me eighteen years ago. "*Saaf chehra chahiye. Bilkul saaf.*" (I want a clean face. Absolutely clean.)

3

The Wisdom of Words and Silences

In the mid-1990s, I went to the United States to pursue higher studies. By now I had already started to admire Dilip Kumar the person, and had built a familial bond with him. I would often enjoy meeting him over lively cups of tea every time I came to India during the summer vacations. It was a tradition of sorts. I cherished these meetings to such an extent that it was becoming difficult for me to wait till the next time we sat together.

The way Sahab spoke to me aroused my curiosity and stimulated me. While he prompted me to discuss everything under the sun, he was also full of questions about my field of expertise, the subjects I was studying at college. This encouraged me and gave me a sense of pride in what I was doing. After all, not everyone has Dilip Kumar asking you about how you are doing with your academic pursuits.

While I had decided to pursue an undergraduate programme in computers and information systems, the beauty of an American college curriculum allowed me to expand my horizons. So apart from the core technical subjects, I dipped

into the fields of philosophy and literature. During one of
my summer visits, Sahab enquired about the courses I had
been pursuing. I briefly mentioned the different classes I was
taking, but the one subject that caught his attention was Greek
philosophy.

"So, you are trying to make sense of Socrates and Plato?"

"Yes, Sahab, but I haven't understood much."

He smiled. Over the next fifteen minutes, Sahab gave me a
crash course on Plato's dialogues and Socrates's views on ethics.
To my surprise, Sahab had an extensive understanding of the
teachings of these two historic thinkers.

Over my many conversations with him I discovered why
people felt mesmerized speaking with him and why it was such
a joy to everyone who was fortunate enough to do that. He
had the uncanny ability to create a personal equation with a
person. It was as if he was attuning himself to the wavelength
of the person in front of him. I understood the reason behind
the pauses his conversations were punctuated with. They
not only allowed the listener to partake of the rich language
but also internalize the thoughts he enunciated. I couldn't
take my eyes off him in those moments. I would be eagerly
waiting for the next words, or be amazed at the astuteness of
his observations. The impact was profound. His words were
few, but they conveyed a deep understanding of the subject.
Dilip Sahab taught me the value of words. What we say is as
important as what we choose not to. As much as we impact
people with what we say, we impact them with our silence too.
It was because of him that I learnt to appreciate words and the
responsibility that comes with our command over them.

Every exchange with him broadened my horizon, my
understanding of the world. Once, he held my hand and said,
"Young man, strive to be a philosopher, but never be a sophist."

I did not understand what he meant.

It was only later in life that I realized how true the statement is. We don't listen to people, yet we are forthright in advising them. We don't hear, but we're always ready with an 'intelligent' solution. We provide specious reasoning in pursuit of what we believe in and expect people to live according to what we articulate. Dilip Sahab taught me something I would probably never have noticed.

For those who knew him up close it was fascinating how he could be reserved and yet accessible at the same time. He was an introvert but he revelled in interacting with others. He liked to keep to himself but at the same time could drive a stimulating conversation well into the night till sleep beckoned. In so many ways he was open with people around him, and yet there was a mystery about him. I often thought of him as a man who taught without seeming to do so. The import of his words would often escape the listener at the time. It was only on solitary reflection that one realized the wisdom of what he had said.

In late 2000, I started my first entrepreneurial venture, MouthShut.com. I had just come back from the US and was ready to make a change in the world. It was around the Internet boom that I started a review website. I wanted to create a platform for consumers where they would have the liberty to relay their experiences with various products and services across the country.

People were very much taken by the website. There was a flood of reviews coming in every day. Brands were getting written about, and sellers were starting to take notice. More and more people flocked to MouthShut.com on a daily basis to read and write reviews. Soon enough, MouthShut.com started gaining traction. We were getting massive media attention for the uniqueness of the website. This went on for quite a few years.

As time went by, the frequency of press coverage and news appearances increased rapidly. My name was increasingly being mentioned with the likes of other successful entrepreneurs and industry experts. I enjoyed sending these newspaper cuttings and VCDs of my interviews to Dilip Sahab for him to read, listen to and offer his feedback. He would often call me back to congratulate me, or to speak to me about the matter.

In 2003, I was invited to Cannes for a global conference on market research as a keynote speaker. Filled with excitement of an invitation to speak at Cannes, I called Dilip Sahab and told him about it.

With a hint of pride in his voice, he asked me, "Is it a tech conference at Cannes?"

"Yes! It's a great platform. And it's a very big opportunity. Do you have any tips for me?"

"I was at Cannes almost half a century ago. The world has changed so much since then. You do your best, and have a safe trip."

The conference went off remarkably well. I came back feeling elated. When I met Sahab, I showed him all the pictures and clips from the conference, and from around Cannes and Nice. He looked at the pictures with curiosity and delight. Then turning to me, he said, "*Aap jo kaam kar rahe hain, yeh bohot achhchha hai. Lekin media ke liye aap rahe rahe gaayab ho jaya kariye.*" (This work that you're doing is very good. But for the media, you should disappear sometimes.)

I was zapped. I didn't fully understand his words. He didn't follow up with any explanation, continuing to browse through the pictures and clips, enjoying himself.

Over time, I realized what he actually meant to say. The world loves a good mystery. Unknowingly, we are attracted to questions we cannot answer. We are a curious race, and the best way to keep people hooked is to be an enigma.

As an entrepreneur and a personality who had plenty of media exposure, I had to find a balance. Dilip Sahab's words made me realize that while it was good to be in the limelight, it was equally important not to lose one's way. A diamond is precious, but it's the blue diamond that holds true value.

His statement rings truer than ever. It is not essential for one to be in front of the media all the time. We have to be there for the right things. When you overexpose yourself to the audience, there is a possibility you might be taken for granted. You lose your sense of privacy, and every action ends up being scrutinized. Over the years, I have applied this rule to myself, and even today, when I'm approached to speak at a conference, gathering, or panel, I ensure that my presence is actually necessary, that the subject is relevant, that they evoke a debate. As the CEO of a company, I try to watch my words with every person I meet. Professionally, when I appear on panels, speak at conferences, or even have an interaction with someone from the industry, I try to use words that can stimulate and inspire. Even if my words cause a stir, it should be for the greater good, not to encourage negativity. Sahab's wise words gave me the opportunity to develop this aspect of my persona. It is from Dilip Sahab that I learnt that when a person leaves you after a conversation, whether or not they remembered the words, they must leave with a feeling of having had a meaningful and respectful interaction.

Dilip Sahab followed these rules strictly. He never shied away from a camera, or turned his back to his fans, but what was happening in his private life was a question very few got an answer to. He would seldom open up about his private life with others. When it came to his fans and the media, he always maintained an arm's-length relationship with them, keeping his answers crisp and to the point. He didn't like promoting himself. As an actor, he promoted his work and the work of the team. He didn't put just himself out there. He didn't indulge in any promotional activity, or become a brand ambassador for any product or service. He would promote his movies, promote charitable organizations, but he ensured that he was never overwhelmed by the media glare. As such, the mystery surrounding him never lifted. Although, like anyone else in the limelight, he couldn't escape the controversies that surrounded him.

One of the most famous controversies surrounding his name involved Madhubala. Reports from the 1950s suggested a love, a relationship, that would culminate into a lifelong commitment of marriage. Sadly, this was not to be. They broke up. Madhubala, regarded by many as the most beautiful actress to grace Indian cinema, was said to be an obedient daughter, stuck between family and love. In the rather famous and vitriolic court case between movie producer B.R. Chopra and Ataullah Khan, Madhubala's father, Dilip Kumar had chosen the righteous path and been a key witness in favour of the Chopras. It is widely known that during his statement, Dilip Sahab had also professed his love for her, but the rest of the words exchanged had been too hurtful for both sides.

With so much said between them, and about them, the world was eagerly waiting to hear their side of the story.

Dilip Sahab never spoke ill about the woman he was once destined to marry. In every interview he gave, he kept mum on the details. There was nothing but respect for Madhubala every time he mentioned her. He wasn't one to dig up old graves. I found that out one evening when I went to meet him.

It was sometime in 2006 and I was sitting with Dilip Sahab at Jogger's Park. The last rays of the setting sun shone a bright red all around us. Sahab and I were enjoying the silence. Earlier that day, an article had been published about him and Madhubala, trashing their love story. It was clear that the article was targeted at gossip-hungry readers. I turned to Sahab and inquired if he had read the article.

"Sahab, *aaj ek article tha aapke aur Madhubala ke bare mein.*" I had rehearsed the question several times in my mind. I had decided to muster the courage and ask him the truth behind the many versions floating about him and Madhubala. People who knew me and my love for Dilip Kumar had often implored me to ask him.

Sahab's face betrayed the slightest trace of irritation.

He looked at me and said, "*Sab bakwaas likhte hain yeh.*" (It's all trash.)

"Why don't you write a rebuttal to this? They shouldn't be able to get away with wrong information just for the sake of publicity."

Did I discern a slight stiffening of his demeanour? He was silent, hand on his face, pondering something deep. His face unnerved me.

Had I crossed a line?

Was I not supposed to ask this question?

Was it not my place?

Had I opened old wounds?

Was Dilip Sahab angry with me?

Would I be asked to leave?

He looked at me with eyes that had witnessed generations. Wise, old and soulful. His tall figure leaned over, and in a flat, but stern tone, he spoke to me.

"Young man," and then a pause, "some things should just go with you to the grave."

As the warm evening grew cool with the breeze, and darkness descended, Dilip Sahab had once again left something lingering. His words, although few, held so much in them. There was complete silence.

When I looked at him again, I felt like the man in front of me didn't want to say anything because he knew that it wasn't anyone else's business. His faraway gaze seemed to be in love with that woman still. Not in the way he loves his wife. Saira Banu is the woman of his life. He loves her deeply and I have seen their love reflected in every conversation, even in the simplest form. What he felt for Madhubala was probably the twitch you feel in your heart when you reminisce about an old friend, or a lover, or someone who was close to you in life. A past that is not quite forgotten. It thrives, it throbs, with every other bittersweet memory.

4

A Curious Mind: Sahab Discovers Amazon, iPhone, YouTube and Twitter

I have never met someone as inquisitive as Dilip Sahab. He was constantly looking to learn and grow. A voracious reader, he was always aware of current affairs and social issues.

Reading is one of the many habits I picked up from him. In school, my reading was restricted to my curriculum and I enjoyed it. But it was only after Dilip Sahab's encouragement that I started reading other books. Dilip Sahab often told me that reading had a significant impact on both his personal and professional life. It had helped him shape his personality, his ideals and become the person he was.

Dilip Sahab read everything – from English crime thrillers to mesmerizing Urdu poetry. He read across genres, across languages. He was like a sponge soaking in the best of prose and poetry from around the world. He had a massive library at his place and every time I visited him, it seemed to have grown a little bigger. If you ever walked into Dilip Sahab's house, you would have seen a wide coffee table sitting proudly among the other furniture in the living room. This table was where all of Sahab's daily newspapers were kept. Dilip Sahab always made it a point to read the daily papers to stay well-informed about current affairs. He would read local, national and international newspapers. That was one of the things I loved about him. He was constantly evolving – by learning new things, expanding his knowledge and widening his horizons to stay relevant with the times.

I think broadly there are two types of readers. The first kind treats reading like a challenge they have to complete. They read multiple books, but seldom retain the information contained in them. Then there's the second kind. Dilip Sahab belonged to the latter category. He read a lot of books, and took his time with each one of them. Every book was a new learning experience for him. He immersed himself into every line. He remembered every book he read. He often quoted the impressive poems and verses he had read. And he quoted them as fluently in English as he would in Urdu.

In the late 1990s, during my college days, Amazon.com had built an impressive global collection of books. Once, when I was busy packing my bags to leave for the US the next day, I received a call from Dilip Sahab. He asked me, "Faisal, I have heard that there is a bookstore in the US where you can find whichever book you want."

"Yes, Sahab. Amazon.com. It's a website. I can order any book in the world, and they will deliver it to my home in a matter of days."

"*Any* book you want?" he queried, a tone of surprise in his voice.

"Yes, Sahab. Any book."

"That's great! In that case, I will give you the names of a few books. Can you find out by when you will receive them?"

"Yes, Sahab. Please tell me."

I logged on to Amazon.com while he dictated the titles. He read out the names of three books, *Raven Stole the Moon* by Garth Stein, *Acts of God: A Novel* by Mary Morris, and *Windfall: A Novel* by James Magnuson. All of them were thrillers published during the mid- and late-1990s. I was surprised to see that Dilip Sahab was aware of these recent releases.

Admirers and Dilip Kumar fans know that Sahab enjoyed Urdu poetry the most. He would often bring up pertinent shers to express his thoughts on a complicated situation. He believed there was a sher (couplet), a misra (poetic line), or a shayari (full poem) for every emotion known to mankind. He could recall and quote from books he had read years ago. He remembered nazms and shers like they were topics of regular everyday conversation.

Urdu poetry is beautiful and thought-provoking though they might seem vague at times. However, once you scratch the surface, they often offer simple answers to many difficult questions. Some poems come bearing the solution to your existential crisis, others give you the courage to face life's challenges. There's an ethereal romance in Urdu shayari. Perhaps that's why Dilip Sahab used to say that Urdu shayari was the reason he fell in love so often, with life itself.

His thirst for knowledge was such that he would always listen to people with an open mind without jumping to conclusions. Every time he came across a new idea, you could see his eyes sparkle. It was as if a child had stumbled upon a shiny new coin. He would research on the new idea, read books about it, pen his own thoughts on it, and evolve his understanding of the situation as he gathered more knowledge.

In 2005, the Value Added Tax (VAT) was officially introduced in Maharashtra. The whole state was abuzz with chatter about what it was, and how it would affect the state's economy. There were debates and protests. Traders all over the state were going on a strike in an attempt to prevent the implementation of VAT. It was a big strike and it made headlines in all the newspapers.

Dilip Sahab, as curious as ever, had asked me my thoughts on VAT. Being an entrepreneur, I had already done my research. I knew how it would affect my business and understood its nitty-gritties. I explained every aspect of the tax to Sahab. We spoke about the advantages and disadvantages, its relevance, and consequences.

Once I was done, I paused for Sahab's response. I was expecting a conclusion he had drawn from all the information. He just smiled.

"If what you're saying is true, there are a lot of benefits of VAT."

He changed the topic after this but knowing him, I knew he would dive deep into the subject to understand it better.

The next time we found ourselves in the middle of a conversation about VAT, Dilip Sahab had a bunch of opinions about it and a lot to say.

He was quite amazed at the advancements in technology, but was also slightly critical of it. He often rued how technology had come at the cost of the quality of human interactions. Sahab shared a funny relationship with technology. He had dictated a couple of blog posts to me. He loved to tweet, often taking a long time to compose a single tweet. However, like any other person of his age, I believe he found technology slightly intimidating.

He had first discussed the Internet with me in 2000. It was just before I had started my company. Sahab called me home one afternoon.

"What exactly is this Internet?"

Being a techie, I was happy that Sahab was approaching me with these questions. Watching his curiosity and enthusiasm, I was more than happy to explain and demystify the mystery that the Internet was to him.

"Sahab, when you join one computer with other computers in the world, that network is known as the Internet."

"Interesting. How do I join them together?"

"Via phones and a device called modem. You can use the phone line to connect your computer with any other computer in the world the same way you can call anyone in the world with your phone. That is, if that computer also has an Internet connection."

Sahab seemed slightly confused. It was a new concept that the youth was mastering, while the elder population was either trying to understand or avoid. Dilip Sahab was among those who were trying to understand. He had a million questions and I was preparing myself to answer them in a manner that would appeal to him.

"Sahab, do you know, with the Internet, you can make a call to the US for free?"

"Free? How?"

"All you have to do is go to a website called Dialpad.com."

"What is a website?"

"A website is a collection of web pages, or media on the Internet."

"It sounds very confusing."

I chuckled. I knew it was, but I was there to help Sahab understand and learn it. I was going to use Dialpad.com as a means to explain it to him.

Dialpad was one of the first popular websites that allowed free long-distance calling within and to the United States.

I pulled out my laptop, connected it to his landline phone and started showing him how the Internet worked.

Sahab asked me to call his sister in Fresno, California. Unfortunately, the time difference meant the phone kept ringing as she did not answer the call. Additionally, Dialpad. com allowed phone calls only within or to the United States of America, so we couldn't call anybody in India.

A few years later, while walking at Jogger's Park, Sahab and I bumped into a man who had been his fan for years. Like any other fan, he had a lot of questions for Sahab.

Sahab seemed rather agitated by the interference. The fan, like thousands of others, probably believed that Sahab had the energy to answer all of his questions. Although Dilip Sahab wanted to be polite to all his fans, he was growing old. He had a limited amount of energy, and with age, his patience had also started to wear thin.

During those days, Rediff, Yahoo and Hotmail were the three most popular platforms for online interactions. Messengers and chats were the 'in' thing, and people took to chatting big time. I suggested to Sahab that we host an interactive session with him on Rediff.com's Q&A. We would make a system to announce that Dilip Kumar will be online once a month and answer as many fan questions as possible.

"You can do it live, or request that your fans send you their questions in advance. In both scenarios, it will be a great opportunity for the audience to connect with Dilip Kumar."

Sahab loved the idea. Unfortunately, after the first day, I couldn't find enough time to keep him interested in the topic, and the idea was left unexplored. What we did do was practice how Sahab would answer these questions. For the next few weeks, I would pose as his fan. I would come up with questions and ask Sahab, and in return, he would try and answer them as best as he could. It became a game for us, and I learnt a lot about him through our Q&A rehearsals.

When Twitter was launched in 2006, it was an instant hit. It was a great platform to share your thoughts and find out what others had to say. Public figures and celebrities joined the platform in hundreds. There were also a bunch of people posing as celebrities, so Twitter came up with a 'blue tick' against the handle as a mark of authenticity of the account. I wanted Dilip Sahab to join Twitter as well, but being a private person, he didn't agree.

By 2009, I had warmed Sahab up to the idea of Twitter, but he finally authorized me to create his account in December 2011. He posted his first tweet on his eighty-ninth birthday. Newspapers across the country celebrated Dilip Kumar's arrival on Twitter. Twitter's Asia Pacific Head Rishi Jaitley personally came down to my office, thanking me for bringing Dilip Kumar to the platform. Sahab was delighted with the tweets he received. I became his official typist. Every time he would want to share a thought, he would ask me to type it out in 140 characters. It is one of the best jobs I've had in my life.

It was thanks to his engagement with Twitter that I discovered one remarkable thing about Dilip Sahab. Up until a point in time, I used to think he knew three to four languages. Then, a tweet disclosed the stunning reality.

A fan once posed a question on Twitter asking Dilip Sahab the number of languages he spoke. He replied, "In Peshawar, we spoke Hindko at home, and I had friends and neighbours from whom I picked up Pashto. My grandfather was a Farsi scholar, and I grew up speaking Farsi with my grandparents. Of course, we all grew up learning Urdu, as it was the popular culture. Since the family shifted to Bombay and subsequently Deolali, I am indebted to the Barnes School for their emphasis on written and spoken English. At Bombay Talkies, I picked up Bengali from Ashok Bhaiya (Ashok Kumar) and S. Mukherjee Sahab. Growing up in cosmopolitan Bombay, you have to be fluent in Hindi, Gujarati and Marathi. It is the local languages spoken."

That's nine languages!

Soon after that, I asked him, "Sahab, what would you consider your mother tongue?"

Without pausing to think, he replied, "Hindko."

His library was full of books in many of these languages, books written in Urdu and English language dominating the shelves.

Towards the end of 2007, the Apple iPhone was launched in India. The colour display took the country by storm. For the first time, you didn't need a keypad to operate a phone. It worked entirely by touch. Everyone wanted the iPhone.

I had purchased the iPhone as well. It was certainly a little miracle. I was hooked.

Every time I had the phone in my hand, I would browse, open apps, and completely immerse myself into it. I would either be trying to understand how the phone worked or keep tinkering with the apps it had. I'd received a few offhand remarks about my addiction to the device. But I just couldn't help it. Being from a technology background, I had to know everything about this machine. I had to implement it in my business. Thanks to the countless apps, the iPhone quickly became the be-all and end-all of my life. I didn't need to turn on my computer for Facebook or YouTube; the iPhone had apps for them. Heck, it even had apps for news.

One evening, while I was sitting with Dilip Sahab and Saira baji on their terrace, my first iPhone in my hand, I thought the tea could wait. The lights of buildings surrounding us was piercing the silence of the darkness. I was browsing YouTube. The sheer number of videos on YouTube were enough to bring out the child in me. I was listening to old Hindi movie soundtracks.

Sahab, sitting beside me, started to shift in his seat. I was busy surfing my phone, and Sahab was expecting a conversation.

Breaking the silence in the crisp evening air, Sahab said, "*Duniya Dilip Kumar se milne aati hai, aur Dilip Kumar se batein karti hai. Aap aate hain aur apne phone mein masroof rehte hain. Humein bhi to bataiye iske bare mein.*" (The world comes to meet Dilip Kumar, and talks with Dilip Kumar. Every time you come, you're busy with your phone. Tell me about it too.)

I looked away from my phone. I had been so engrossed in my phone that I hadn't realized I was coming across as rude.

"No, no, Sahab," I said sheepishly. "I was watching a few videos on my phone. Sahab, you can talk on this, you can send a message, and you can watch any song that you want."

"*Bakwaas kar rahe ho!*" (That's nonsense!)

Dilip Sahab always used the word 'bakwaas' whenever he wanted to express extreme joy or displeasure. In either case, whenever he used that word, I knew that he was touched by our conversation. It was the one word that I often wished to hear from him during our conversations. There was so much love in that simple word.

"*Nahin, Sahab, aap yeh dekhiye.*" (No, Sahab, watch this.)

I quickly tapped on the YouTube search bar and looked for the song '*Ae Mere Dil Kahin Aur Chal*'. It was a famous song from his 1952 movie, *Daag*. I tapped on the 'play' button and handed the phone to Sahab.

As the video began, a look of amazement spread over Sahab's face. He had never seen anything like this before. He turned to me and said, "Play that other song."

I realized that Sahab wanted to test the limits of this new platform. I asked him which song he wished to listen to, and to my pleasant surprise, he said '*Dhoondo Re Sajna More Kaan Ka Bala*'. It was picturized on Dilip Kumar and Vyjayanthimala in the super-hit movie *Ganga Jumna*, released in 1961. A smile lit up Saira baji's face. I was now the unofficial VJ for the evening.

I played the song for him.

Even today, after more than a decade, I remember the smile that spread across his face. There are only two words that can describe what Dilip Sahab was feeling in that moment – pure joy! In that moment, Dilip Sahab transformed into a child who had found a new toy. He had an ear-to-ear smile as he listened to the song that he had worked so hard for almost half a century ago. He was humming along with the song. Saira baji leaned back in her chair, enjoying her husband's glee as the evening passed us by.

Watching them so happy made me happy too. It was one of those moments where you don't remember every detail of what was happening, but the essence of the moment remains with you forever. It touches a part of your soul, and you just know that you will never forget that moment.

I will never forget the glow on Dilip Sahab's face as he hummed along with the song, smiling to himself. I don't remember what we were doing before that moment, or when I finally left for home. But I will never forget how it felt as we sat there, listening to old songs, Sahab reminiscing about his acting days.

That was the first time he called my phone '*jaadu*' (magic).

Over the years, he went on to repeat that. "This device you have in your hand is magic. Take good care of it," he would often tell me.

When I think of Dilip Sahab, I invariably think of a child. He had the same innocent curiosity as that of a young boy trying to figure out how the world works. He never let go of this inquisitiveness. He always questioned, always opened himself to new possibilities. That's one of the most important lessons I learnt from him – never lose your childlike nature.

It's important to question everything around us. Every day we face situations and new discoveries. Every incident has a meaning behind it. In a way, when I fiddled with the iPhone back in 2008, I was embodying Dilip Sahab's nature. I was curious to know more about this device he so lovingly called jaadu. I wanted to know how it worked, the software used in it, what could be done to further upgrade it, among many other questions. I wanted to learn, and eventually make it a part of my work.

I have tried to keep this inquisitiveness alive every step of the way. In every facet of life, I have questioned, learned, and kept an open mind. I believe that if each one of us adopted this quality, we as humans would not only be successful, but also a more accepting race. We would be open to understanding people, situations, and letting go of petty grudges.

Openness invites a space of comfort and communication. Be it at home, or at the workplace, with friends, or with someone you just met on the road. Curiosity, openness and acceptance create a brighter environment. They make people feel like they're being heard. It shows concern. It shows that you want to learn, and that you care. And that's another lesson I imbibed from Sahab.

5

From Peshawar to Bombay

Dilip Sahab firmly believed that childhood experiences and environment have a deep impact on how a person turns out in later years. Sahab used to stress on the importance of positivity during a child's formative years.

He often narrated instances from his early life and how interactions with his family and friends shaped his thought process when he stepped out independently. When he recounted these stories, he always seemed to drift off into a world of his own. He used to relate many things in his life to his childhood, and he loved talking about it too.

He would often wander off trying to remember the 'good old days'. He has recalled in depth, in his autobiography, *The Substance and The Shadow*, the simpler times before he was a star, before he was introduced to the world of cinema.

My conversations with him – about his home, school, and how he grew up to be the man I knew – were an attempt to learn from him, rather than to interview him. He often filled the pauses between conversations by narrating stories from his childhood.

Dilip Kumar, then called Muhammad Yusuf Khan, was born on the morning of 11 December 1922 in Peshawar, a city in North-West Frontier Province or Khyber Pakhtunkhwa, now in Pakistan, then British India. He was born in a large joint family and had six brothers and five sisters. In the words of Dilip Sahab, "There was never a quiet or dull moment." His grandparents, aunts and uncles and cousins also lived with them. Every day was a new adventure of sorts.

Dilip Sahab's initial years were spent in Peshawar. His dadaji (paternal grandfather) was a prominent personality in the social circles of Peshawar and the North-West Frontier Province. Sahab's father, Lala Ghulam Sarwar Khan, was a businessman, a fruit merchant, who owned orchards in Peshawar, and later in Deolali near Nashik (in present-day Maharashtra). A large part of his business was conducted in Bombay, at the city's famous Crawford Market. In Bombay, he earned the love and friendship of many literary and religious scholars, freedom fighters and professionals of his time. He was also the first to introduce rare dry fruits to the city, which were especially grown in the North-West Frontier Province. He would transport fruits to other metropolitan markets, but operated primarily between Peshawar and Bombay.

Dilip Kumar enjoyed his childhood. Being a naughty, outdoorsy boy, he got into a lot of trouble with his paternal grandmother. Even as a young boy, Sahab loved stories. He would often sit with his grandfather who was an excellent storyteller. Sahab would intermittently tell me about the flair with which his grandfather would narrate tales of princes, religious figures, heroes, and wonderlands, subtly hinting at wisdom hidden in each of them.

I used to picture my own mother during these conversations. Growing up, I was lucky to have heard such beautiful tales from her. Today, when I talk about her, my eyes tear up. Grandparents have so much love to give. Their stories, their scolding, their bounty, in the end, it's all for the grandchildren.

In Peshawar, Sahab's grandmother, for all intents and purposes, was the household matriarch. Dilip Sahab often told me how everyone feared her. Her word would be what Sahab called, 'patthar ki lakeer' (set in stone).

"My grandmother was very strict."

"So, you must have been scared of her?"

"*Everyone* at home was scared of her."

Peshawar was the gateway or the frontier of British India. The British India government had a strong hold on the people, and oppression wasn't a rarity. The independence movement was gaining momentum at the time. Mohandas Gandhi had assumed the Congress leadership, and in a few pockets, people were starting to take up arms against the Raj in the form of civil disobedience. Protests and clashes were ubiquitous.

Dilip Sahab would narrate to me stories about the strength his grandparents displayed in the face of such adversity. Sahab would often be chided for his feckless wanderings. This once led him to an event which I don't think he ever forgot. He brought it up after our evening walk one day.

I often accompanied Sahab to Jogger's Park, where we would enjoy nice strolls every now and then. On one such evening, we were perched on a bench. The sea shone beautifully, dancing with the colours of the sky. At a distance, a small group of children were running around, probably on a sugar rush after having cotton candy from the vendor nearby. Their mothers were trying to calm them down. An innocent sight bathed in the warm evening light.

Dilip Sahab turned to me and said, "*Aksar, bachpan ke waaqyat bohot gehre tassuraat chhod jaate hain. Wajood ki soorat kabhi yaksa nahin rehti.*" (Often, childhood experiences leave a profound impact. Life doesn't remain the same after that.)

It was a rather heavy statement considering the peaceful ambience around us. His solemn words were a contrast to the warmth of the evening. He paused. I looked at him intently, waiting for him to elucidate on his statement. There was only silence on his part.

You're right, I said, in an attempt to end the silence. His pause lasted longer than usual. There was a faraway look in his eyes. Like he was lost somewhere. He cocked his head to one side, looked towards me, and continued, "I was quite young, perhaps eight years old. You can say I was a bit mischievous too. I would often wander off with kids from my neighbourhood."

He paused briefly once again, and then recalled to me a short incident that left me aghast.

Word by word, he created a portrait of Qissa Khwani Bazaar, where his ancestral home still stands. He spoke about a small community of peaceful people, busy in their daily lives, and a boy merely eight years old. Every evening, Sufis and scholars, wandering traders and friendly soldiers would narrate stories of travel and valour, of loss and grief, of kindness and love, of good and evil, of loyalty and deceit. For a little while every evening, the people of Qissa Khwani Bazaar would get transported into a brand-new world.

As a young boy, Dilip Sahab seldom stayed home. One hot afternoon, while roaming the bustling lanes of Qissa Khwani Bazaar with two other friends, they noticed something out of the ordinary. A short distance away, a crowd was forming. There were people gathering. What started as a buzz soon turned into a loud hum. It was the sound of the masses gathering for a protest. The civil disobedience movement had been gathering momentum and the number of peaceful protests across the country had increased several fold. Dilip Sahab and his friends had stumbled upon one such protest.

The three young boys watched as people silently stood against the British Raj. Soon, a low rumble could be heard at a distance. It was the sound of the army approaching. There was a palpable unease in the crowd of protesters.

Sahab was grim. I could see an image haunting his eyes as he continued to narrate the incident to me that day, seventy years after it happened.

When the army approached, they opened fire on the congregation without warning. It was abrupt. It was quick. People started dropping to the ground as soon as the bullets started flying. The sound was deafening, the screams horrifying.

Young Yusuf panicked and rushed to find shelter. He and one of his friends found asylum in an abandoned room. From behind a rickety furniture, they could see the horror unfold. It was surreal to say the least. Scores of people clutched their religious amulets and uttered the Lord's name, feeble but proud voices saying 'Allah-u-Akbar' (The Lord is Great), as they slumped to the ground.

The protesters were unarmed. Their only protection was their Lord, but young Yusuf had never seen such courage. They were surrendering themselves to their Lord, standing true to their beliefs and their love for the motherland. Not one person tried to retaliate. Not one person reached for a weapon. Not one person attacked the soldiers. They welcomed death with open arms.

It was probably Dilip Sahab's most profound childhood memory. He told me that the incident changed him forever. As he finished his story, he told me how scared he was.

"I couldn't shut my eyes, and I couldn't watch. I had frozen."

With a slight tremble in his voice, Sahab continued. He told me how he could see the bullets tearing through flesh. It was his first encounter with death. The incident haunted him for years.

When he got back home, he didn't speak to anyone for three whole days. The boy who always loved being outside, no longer wanted to leave the safety within the four walls of his home. In a large extended family with numerous children, no one really noticed the change in his behaviour. I believe this probably added to the trauma. For children, it is essential that they be able to share their experiences, especially the negative ones, with others – parents and other elders in the family – who can provide the child with comfort and probably even an explanation.

"I have had nightmares ever since that incident. It plays in my head like a movie," he said.

Sahab's words resonated with me. I couldn't imagine the terror he must have felt. A young boy, full of life, watching life cruelly drained out of so many people. It is a trauma only a few can cope with.

I suddenly looked at the children playing nearby, and this time, looked at them from a whole new perspective. With all my heart, I prayed that no child has to face the horrors of war and violence. All over the world, children are being orphaned, leading traumatic lives as they grow up.

Sahab had taken about twenty minutes to narrate the incident, yet after so many years, I have not been able to forget it. I thank the Lord that neither I, nor my children, have witnessed anything like this. It changes a person fundamentally. Sahab was right. Childhood experiences leave traces that remain throughout people's lives.

A few weeks later, I was wondering why I had not heard of this gruesome incident earlier. I had not read about it in any book or article. So, I Googled the event. I put in a few keywords and after a brief search, found the incident. It's called the 'Qissa Khwani Bazaar Massacre of 1930'.

The protest that led to the massacre was inspired by Khan Abdul Ghaffar Khan, also called the Frontier Gandhi. 'I'm going to give you such a weapon that neither the police nor the army will be able to stand against it. It is the weapon of the Prophet, but you are not aware of it. The weapon is patience and righteousness. No power on earth can stand against it," Khan Abdul Ghaffar Khan had said and the crowd at Qissa Khwani Bazaar had obeyed him even as the British forces opened fire on them.

Dilip Sahab always preferred to keep to himself. His need for privacy could be a result of the trauma he experienced as a child. Having no one to speak with after the incident, he found solace in his mother a few months later, when she asked him what was bothering him.

Soon after, Sahab and his siblings, along with their parents, moved to Bombay's Nagdevi area near Mohammad Ali Road area where his father had already established himself as a successful fruit trader in the nearby Crawford Market.

Upon hearing about his family's upcoming trip to Bombay, young Yusuf was unable to hold back his excitement. He didn't know at that time that he would be moving to the city of dreams permanently. Dilip Sahab told me that his initial years in Bombay were a mix of good and bad. He loved the pace at which the city moved. It was like someone had forgotten to install a pause button. On the other hand, the polluted air only worsened his mother's and brother's health. They were both diagnosed with asthma quite early on. The pollution in the city didn't do anything to ease that either.

Sahab was always very close to his mother. Her slim petite frame, and sharp smiling features are something he often spoke about. Around the year 2002, I was at Sahab's home with him. We were sipping tea in his garden. I was talking to Sahab about my mother. My family was my biggest support when I was starting my venture, and my mother's love was incomparable. Sahab, ever engrossed in the conversation, told me how every mother in the world is so loving.

"Every mother lives only for her children. And then there is my mother..."

As soon as those words escaped his lips, he became teary eyed. One small droplet balanced on his lower eyelash for a while, and ever so lightly, made its way down his cheek. I was speechless. I had never seen him this emotional, never witnessed him with tears in his eyes.

His mind had drifted off into a world where he was still a child, holding his mother close. After a brief pause, he continued, "She is the most beautiful woman I have ever seen. Even today, her absence brings tears to my eyes. As a child, I never thought I would live in a world where my mother did not exist."

The atmosphere turned sombre. Despite all those years without her, he still remembered her as the loving and caring woman she was. Sahab loved talking about his mother, and amid the sombre ambience and prolonged pauses, he opened his heart to me. He shared the love that still lived in his heart for his mother.

Ayesha Begum was a pragmatic and courageous woman. Always on her feet, she worked right till the end. She made sure that her kids grew up respectful and obedient. She would never compromise on their education, moral or institutional.

In his warm beige room at Pali Hill, there was a beautiful photo of his mother, one copy of which adorned the bedside table, and one that was perched proud in the living room. Often, when I visited him, and we would sit chatting, he would point at his mother's photo and sombrely say, "*Humaari Amma*" (My mother).

His demeanour used to change when he spoke of his mother. Suddenly, he would turn into this boy, huddled in his mother's arms, missing her embrace, her voice, her smell. As he looked at his mother's photo, I used to look at him. That's the most vulnerable I have ever seen him.

When I used to meet him in the absence of guests, he usually wore a white kurta and a plain-white lungi. He used to drape a beige shawl and sit on his comfortable sofa, leaning on one side, his face balanced on just a few fingers, and his elbow digging into the armrest, creating a crease in the leather.

He would gingerly raise his other hand, and point to his mother's picture.

Her picture was truly captivating. Dilip Sahab once told me how he would marvel at his mother, and her beauty.

"She was so petite, but so strong. Always doing something. Always scurrying about. She worked every single day of her life. My mother took care of all her children. Always the beloved and loyal wife. She and Aghaji (father) never had a conversation in raised voices."

"Do you miss her?"

"Every day."

He said it with a slight smile. Eyes deep and filled to the brim with a million emotions swimming in them. He would never forget the woman who raised him.

"I was never too keen on working in the film industry. I just had one wish. That my father gets some help in running the household, and my mother gets some rest."

Dilip Sahab's mother was the reason why every home they lived in remained beautiful and always filled with laughter and joy. She took care of everyone. His parents taught them the

Pathan values of strength and pride, of grace and hospitality, and inculcated in them respect for others and for education. Breaking from conventions of the time, Aghaji emphasized on formal education for his children. With every travel or move, Aghaji ensured that his children would be taken care of with respect to education and health.

Their initial stay in Bombay was rather brief. Given the poor health his mother and brother were keeping, they decided to move to Deolali, a small town about 160 km from Bombay. Due to their severe asthma, the doctor had suggested a change of location. Sahab's father owned a small orchard in Deolali, so moving to the new town was not a difficult task. Deolali had the kind of weather that Aghaji thought was best for his wife and son.

It was in Deolali that Sahab received his most significant education. He was accepted into Barnes School. Growing up, Sahab learnt various languages. It was English that he extensively used. It helped him during his initial days in his career prior to his entry into the world of Indian cinema.

Dilip Sahab would tell me how indebted he was to Barnes School.

"What I learnt there helped me build my life. The school's teaching and discipline were exceptional. Their personal attention and focus helped me a lot."

At Barnes, Sahab learnt fluent English. He was introduced to elocution, poetry, storytelling, and many other co-curricular activities. His love for the classics grew. He was introduced to books like *Jane Eyre*, *Moby Dick*, and *War and Peace*. He credits part of his grace and knowledge to this school.

Unfortunately, before he could complete his matriculation, they moved back to Bombay. Sahab completed his matriculation from Anjuman Islam School, at VT in

Bombay, and intermediate exam from Khalsa College in Matunga, Bombay, where he enjoyed playing cricket and football. His talent on the football field earned him a direct scholarship at Wilson College, Chowpatty, Bombay. He was selected in the professional football team at Wilson and the principal was certain that he would lead their team to great victories soon.

"Life took an abrupt turn then," said Sahab to me while describing his college days. There was tremendous pressure at home to support the family's dwindling financial resources. With the Second World War raging in Europe and the Far East, the struggles with British India's rail and road transport were only increasing. Dilip Sahab's father owned as well as leased orchards in Peshawar and Deolali, and transported them via rail to various fruit markets throughout India. During the War, the wagons that once carried delicious fruits were now being used for arms, ammunition, and military transport. The fruits that would be sold in cities were now rotting in the orchards, and with no place to go, and with dwindling sales, Sahab's father faced extreme financial crunch. More and more businesses and people were suffering, and so was Lala Ghulam Sarwar Khan's Peshawar-Bombay fruit business.

One day, he had a mild altercation with his father. Everyone at home was expecting him to pull his weight, and finally something just snapped. In a huff, Dilip Sahab packed his bags and left home. He travelled to Pune where he began his journey as another earning member of the family.

Whenever Sahab spoke to me about his childhood, I used to relate it to mine.

Dilip Sahab never told me how to behave, but his stories made me introspect and assess my own behaviour and environment. I'm a firm believer that our relationship with our parents defines our relationship with our children. It is a deep-rooted ideology that is unshaken, and the biggest truth I know.

I am a strong believer that what you do, your children pick up. Sometimes, we don't even realize the repercussions of a simple statement we must have made. Even basic things like picking up our plates when we're done with food inculcates a good sense of responsibility in the children. Our experiences from childhood are the ink with which the stories of our lives are written. It's important to write carefully.

6

Early Career and Birth of an Actor

Every time I needed advice on work, Dilip Kumar told me one thing. "If Muhammad Yusuf Khan can become a movie actor, anybody can become a movie actor. You should keep working hard, you'll anyway get your reward."

Dilip Sahab started working following an altercation with his father, but stuck to it to lend a helping hand to his family. Leaving college midway, he didn't have a plan in mind when he went to Pune. He knew he had to find work. He knew he had to earn. He knew he had to be self-reliant. He knew he had to support a large family of many siblings, an ailing mother and a father whose business was facing tough times.

His first job involved working for the British Army Cantonment canteen in Pune. He didn't take long to start managing the canteen and become a favourite among the army officers. His excellent command over English earned him appreciation from everyone he interacted with. They were dazzled by the young boy from a humble background speaking with such fluency.

At the cantonment, he came in contact with an officer who was impressed with not only his English, but also his work ethic. He noticed that unlike others, Yusuf Khan put in extra efforts as a worker in the canteen. He didn't manage the canteen from the perspective of making money. He handled it according to what the customers needed. In the eyes of the officer, that was one of the most important traits a man could have.

He lent a supporting hand to Sahab, and with his help, Sahab opened his own canteen. He had the skills, ideas, and a two-year lease.

It's during this time that Sahab became a culinary savant of sorts. He learnt the art of making the perfect cup of tea, and the most delicious sandwiches. His canteen boasted a mouth-watering menu.

When his lease was up, he returned to Bombay in mid-1943 with a chunk of savings. Although it was a substantial amount, Sahab required an additional steady income to help his father run the household. He started looking for a job.

One day, he came across an advertisement for sales personnel for a pillow importer's store at Charni Road. Dilip Sahab wanted to start a pillow business and a good job experience would come in handy before he started his own company, so he decided to try for the job. On his way to the interview, Dilip Sahab was at the Churchgate station, waiting for the train to Charni Road, when life took one of its unfathomable turns.

Little did he know then that his life would never be the same again.

"*Kuch misaalein zindagi mein ittefaqan hoti hain lekin agar woh na hoti, toh zindagi bohot mukhtalif hoti. Hum kitne mukhtalif hote.*" (Some things in life happen by chance. But for them, life would be so different. We would be so different.)

He added, "I was out looking for a job, and look where life took me."

As Dilip Sahab stood waiting for his train, he heard someone call out to him, "Yusuf!"

Sahab turned around. At a distance, he saw their family friend, Dr Masani, walking towards him through the crowd. Dressed to the nines, he looked like he was doing well in life.

"Yusuf mian. As'salamalaikum," he said, as he greeted Dilip Sahab with a warm hug. Sahab, happy to run into him at the station, replied with a warm smile, "Walaikumsalam."

"Where are you headed so early in the morning?" Dr Masani asked.

"Just out looking for a job. Finished with an interview for a position at Bombay House (headquarters of the Tata Group). Now headed to Charni Road for another interview."

"Looking for a job?" Dr Masani asked. He paused for a bit and then said, "I have an opportunity for you. Come with me. It's a good job, and the pay will be decent."

Dilip Sahab's face lit up. "Of course. Where do we have to go?"

"We'll take the train to Malad. To a studio. I'll introduce you to the people there and you'll get a job."

Back in 1943, Malad, a small distant suburb, north of the city of Bombay, comprised nothing but forest land and a few small villages. It was a remote location and people seldom travelled to Malad. It was populated with countless farms on one end, and a rough sea towards the west. Most of Bombay in 1943 was concentrated in what is now known as South Bombay – from Colaba to Mahim. The suburbs to the other side of the Mithi river beyond Mahim were small villages, and few people lived in these areas.

The twenty-one-year-old Yusuf Khan and Dr Masani reached Malad and stopped in front of the large gates that read 'Bombay Talkies'. The gates looked intimidating to him. Sahab had hardly ever watched a movie, and he had never imagined himself working in the film industry. He just wanted a job to help sustain his household.

He walked in with Dr Masani, who told him they were going to meet the studio's owner, Devika Rani. Bombay Talkies was built over a huge area. The grandness of the premises left Dilip Sahab enchanted.

Devika Rani was a force to reckon with. She was the First Lady of Indian Cinema. A film-maker and a popular actor in the 1930s and early 1940s, she was married to an equally accomplished film-maker, Himanshu Rai. Both avid film buffs, the couple had taken training in Germany to hone their skills. They were among the pioneers in the Indian film industry. Together, they started a full-fledged studio, Bombay Talkies, to give life to Indian cinema as we know it today.

In the early 1940s, Bombay Talkies was the only studio in India with top-of-the-line equipment. It was set up to not only match international standards, but also as a platform for artists to experiment and take the art of cinema further. Devika Rani's husband, Himanshu Rai, unfortunately had a short life. After his untimely demise, she took over the studio, and ran it for the next few decades.

Known for her socially conscious movies, she was termed as the 'Dragon Lady' by Tilak Rishi in his book *Bless You Bollywood: A Tribute to Hindi Cinema on Completing 100 Years*. It was under her reign that Bombay Talkies emerged as a leading player in the Indian film industry. Her studio served as a launch pad for some of the great successes of the era, such as Ashok Kumar, Raj Kapoor, Mumtaz, Madhubala, and Muhammad Yusuf Khan, aka Dilip Kumar.

As Yusuf Khan entered Devika Rani's huge office, he noticed the contrast between her strong posture and the delicate features of her face. She was a beauty to say the least. She turned to notice the young man walking towards her. She had a cigarette in one hand, her red lips perfectly curving around the brown stick as she inhaled, and her other hand resting casually on her delicate waist. As she exhaled the smoke, the grey mist created a cloud of mystery that gingerly wrapped itself around her. Dilip Sahab had never met a woman so bold and confident.

Devika Rani smiled, slightly shifting her gaze as she watched her friend, Dr Masani, approaching. They embraced, and then he proceeded to introduce the young Yusuf Khan to her. As Sahab stepped forward to greet her, Devika Rani looked at him intently.

"You're here looking for a job? What do you want to do?"

"I'm looking for a job with a decent pay," Dilip Sahab said. "I have a large family and I cannot afford to remain unemployed. I am ready for whatever work you deem fit for me."

Have you ever done any work in a film or acted in a drama or play?" Devika Rani asked him, giving him the once over, from the top of his thick lustrous hair, his manners, his soft mellow voice, to his polished but noticeably mangy shoes.

"Come back tomorrow," Devika Rani said.

Dilip Sahab was delighted. He thanked Dr Masani and took the train back home to Churchgate, nervous but excited that he may finally have a job.

He didn't know it then, but it was an opportunity of a lifetime. I wondered what must have been going through his mind while on his way back home.

"What was running through your mind on the way back home?" I asked him when he was narrating the story to me.

"I was praying that I find a decent job in some writing or research department at Bombay Talkies."

The next day, when he returned to Bombay Talkies, he was not accompanied by Dr Masani. He was an unknown man, randomly trying to walk into a reputed studio. He was greeted by a scrawny watchman with a big moustache.

"Yes?" he said when he saw Dilip Sahab at the gate.

"I've come to meet Devika Rani for a job."

Visibly shocked, the guard said, "Huh! This is Bombay Talkies! You think anyone who wants a job is allowed to enter?" He repeated the name 'Bombay Talkies' a few more times. He may have wanted to stress on just how important and fancy the studio really was.

Sahab, patient as ever, handed over the business card Dr Masani had given him the previous day after his meeting with Devika Rani. The guard seemed a little more stunned now. He asked Sahab to wait outside while he checked with the management.

Dilip Sahab waited at the entrance.

"Yeah, go in," the guard said when he returned.

The very same day, as Sahab exited the large gates of the studio, he had a job. For two days, Yusuf Khan did not show up at work. He had assumed that the salary of Rs 1,200 per month offered to him was too good to be true. Dr Masani came home and asked him to take up the job. He confirmed that the salary was indeed per month and not per annum and he was being offered the position of a lead actor at Bombay Talkies and would be cast in an upcoming movie. And thus began his cinema career.

Having watched only two movies (one was a documentary) until then, Yusuf Khan's new job was going to need a lot of hard work.

His first movie, *Jwar Bhata*, starring Kamini Kaushal opposite him, released in November 1944. Sahab once asked me to do some research and see if any copy or prints of this movie were available. I'm yet to find one.

7

Yusuf to Dilip Kumar: The Slap

The renowned film actor/director Raj Kapoor was a close friend of Dilip Sahab from his days in Peshawar. They remained friends lifelong.

Sahab would often tell me, "We were more than just friends. We were comrades, we were brothers. Our families were close from our days in Peshawar. Both Raj and I started out in the film industry almost at the same time. He was assisting a director at Bombay Talkies when I started as an actor. I was happy I knew at least one person when I started my acting career."

Raj Kapoor was the grandson of Dewan Basheswarnath Kapoor. Fondly called Lala Basheswarnath, he and Dilip Sahab's father, Lala Ghulam Sarwar Khan, were almost of the same age and close friends. Lala Basheswarnath's eldest son, Prithviraj, married early and thus his son Raj Kapoor and Dilip Kumar had an age difference of only two years, Sahab being the older one.

Lala Ghulam Sarwar considered the arts field frivolous. He would often talk about Prithviraj, who was heading a popular theatre group, to Lala Basheswarnath. "Why does Prithvi need to get involved in theatres, dramas and plays? He is an able lad, he is talented. Tell him to look for a good job somewhere else. He has a wife and kids. He's young. There's still time. Tell him to get a grip on his life."

Lala Basheswarnath would chuckle, shake his head, and let it go. He knew his friend meant well. In his heart, Lala Ghulam Sarwar only cared about Prithviraj. It's strange, the ironies of life. Lala Ghulam Sarwar had never imagined that his own son would one day not only join but also excel in the industry he so despised.

One evening at Jogger's Park, Dilip Sahab was reminiscing about the time he had taken up acting. Sahab had not yet informed his family about his new job. He knew his father's thoughts on his line of work. If not for the handsome salary, he probably would not have joined the industry.

Sahab told me, "I had never dreamt of becoming an actor. Neither had I imagined a career in films, nor was I a fan of any movie star. I would see my mother and father struggle every day to put food on the table. Amma would save whatever little money my father got home. Despite her frail health, she would scurry from one room to the other, cook food, get the children ready for school, manage the home. When I was offered an in-hand salary of Rs 1,200 a month, I had to take it. Back in the 1940s that was a huge amount. When I had gone to Devika Rani for the job, I was expecting a desk job of some sort, with a pay somewhere around two to three hundred rupees. Maybe Rs 350 rupees a month if I got lucky. I was shocked at the offer they gave me. And humbled at the salary."

He had a smile that shone in his eyes as he paused to ask me if we had by now completed five or six rounds of Jogger's Park. Remembering those early days only brought joy to Dilip

Sahab. As we continued our walk, Sahab continued his trip down memory lane.

"Amma would always ask me how I was bringing home so much money. She made me swear that I wasn't involved in any wrongdoing."

Devika Rani was aware of Dilip Kumar's conservative background and his own reluctance regarding the film industry. At a meeting at Bombay Talkies she offered Yusuf Khan a chance to select a stage name for himself. The options given were: Vasudev, Jahangir Khan and Dilip Kumar. Yusuf required a stage name only because he didn't want his father to find out about his acting career, so he told the production house that he was all right with any of the names suggested.

When the first promotional poster of the movie came out, it read: '*Jwar Bhata*. Starring Dilip Kumar'. It was through this poster that Sahab came to know of his stage name. Comically, it was misspelled quite often as 'Dileep Kumar' during the early days.

The beautiful hand-painted posters looked so good that I often wondered why the artists who painted them weren't given as much attention as other artists. The renowned painter M.F. Husain would often paint movie posters to supplement his earnings in the late 1930s-'40s. As a child, I'd be mesmerized by how well the artists captured the emotions of the actors in these posters.

A number of posters of *Jwar Bhata* were plastered on a wall near the Gulshan-e-Iran Restaurant on the southern end of Mohammad Ali Road, and more were being painted next door at Crawford Market by one of the hard-working painters. Lala Basheswarnath and Lala Ghulam Sarwar Khan, tired from the day's work, were happily on their way back home in a tonga when they spotted one of these posters. The following conversation ensued. I have used the actual words Sahab narrated to me in original Hindko, the language of the Khans and Kapoors from Peshawar.

Flummoxed, Lala Basheswarnath exclaimed, "*Lale, ay poster tay tak. Ay apray Yusuf har nienga?*" (Lale! Look at this poster. Doesn't the face resemble our Yusuf?)

Walking towards the poster, Lala Ghulam Sarwar Khan replied, "*Ai kinj ho sakda ae. Ay tay kisi film da poster ay. Mera putar kisi film day poster tay kyun hosi.*" (How can this be? This is some film's poster. How can my son be on a movie poster?)

Lala Basheswarnath muttered a 'hmm' in agreement. As they both came closer, Lala Basheswarnath noticed the stark similarities between the face on another poster of *Jwar Bhata* and his friend's young handsome boy. Almost amused now, he added, "*Tu tak ta sai, ay Yusuf har e ay. Bary ay thaly naa kisda ay? Dileep Kumar! Lagda ay, aye koi hor e ay.*" (Look at it. He definitely looks like our Yusuf. But what's the name written here below? Dileep Kumar! This is probably someone else.)

Lala Ghulam Sarwar stood there looking at the second poster and didn't utter a word. He saw the resemblance too.

Lala Basheswarnath continued, "Anyway, let it be. Let's leave. I'm shocked how similar that guy on the poster looks to Yusuf. They seem to be of similar age as well. You have a very handsome son, Lale. You wait and watch, someday he'll find a bride as beautiful as the moon."

Lala Ghulam Sarwar smiled at his friend's compliments. He showed his gratitude without equivocation. His face, though, spoke a different language. His smile was tight-lipped, and didn't seem to reach his eyes. He was in a hurry to get back home.

Once home, he marched straight to his room without a word to anyone. He called out his wife's name from his room in a loud voice. When she came to him, he asked, "Where's Yusuf?"

Dilip Sahab's mother, taken aback by her husband's mood, replied, "He is at work. He should be reaching home soon."

"Tell him to come and meet me as soon as he's home."

Ayesha Begum was now curious, and slightly worried. She wondered what her son had done to elicit such a strong reaction from his father. She felt it had something to do with his line of work, one that was paying so well.

Dilip Sahab reached home after a long day of work. All he wanted to do was have dinner and go off to sleep. Maybe sit with Amma for a while. Talking to her after a long, tiring day was surprisingly rejuvenating.

"Yusuf, meet your father once you've freshened up. He seems quite angry. You haven't done anything, have you?"

Dilip Sahab had no idea why his father would be angry. He was quite sure there was no way he would have found out about his 'job'. He quickly freshened up and went to his father's room.

He knocked on his door gingerly and asked if he could enter.

"Come in," came the reply, in quite a grim voice.

Yusuf entered the dimly lit room. On any other night, it would have seemed warm and welcoming. Tonight, it sang a different tune. There was a wide, dark wood bed against the wall. Its intricate design seemed menacing in the dancing yellow glow. The mosquito net fell effortlessly from above, covering the bed in its entirety. It swished gently in the breeze coming from the window, casting more shadows than Yusuf was comfortable with. On the left, there was an equally heavy chair, with a heavier desk in front of it. Yusuf's father usually tended to his work on that table. His pens and books were arranged systematically, probably by Amma. She always believed that a clean space invited higher productivity.

The room seemed to dwarf Yusuf. His father, on the other hand, appeared tall. His shadow towered over the entire room.

He was pacing lightly in front of his desk. He slowed down and then came to a stop as Sahab entered the room and took his place in front of his father.

Yusuf knew something was wrong.

"Assalama'alaikum," said Yusuf to break the silence. His father took a deep breath and replied, "Walaikumsalam."

The silence returned.

Finally, he said, "*Yusuf. Aaj mere nal bari ajeeb jai gal hoi ay. Main dada pareshan han.*" (Yusuf, something strange happened today. I am a bit worried.)

Dilip Sahab, still clueless about why his father was so serious, tried to meet his gaze. There were a million thoughts racing through his head. Had there been an unfortunate incident at his place of work? Was his father angry because of an altercation with a customer or probably with someone in their locality? Or maybe his father just wanted his help on a matter he wasn't able to get out of.

After another brief silence, his father continued, "*Main Lala day nal tangay tay ayain jadon meinay o poster wekha si.*" (I was with Lala on the tonga, and on the way, I saw a film poster.)

Dilip Sahab felt his shoulders tense up and his hands clench behind his back. He was so sure they wouldn't find out about his little secret.

"*Usday uttay kisi Dileep Kumar na day nady thi photo ai. Allah di kasmay o bilkul tery har si.*" (There was some boy named Dileep Kumar on the poster. I swear by Allah, he looked exactly like you.)

Yusuf could feel his heart thumping in his chest like it would burst out any second.

"*Achchaa?*" is all he could muster.

Lala Ghulam Sarwar looked at his son for the first time that evening. He didn't utter a word, just looked at him for a while. The tall Pathan was angry, and torn at what he might find out about his son. Lala Ghulam Sarwar respected Prithviraj immensely. He held his friend's son in high regard. He was tall, good looking and intelligent. But he had different dreams for his own son. He wanted his son to study, and work in a respectable office. Maybe become a lawyer. Start his own practice. As a father, he thought his son was meant for a higher place.

"*Yusuf woh tu ayn poster tay?*" (Yusuf. Was that you on that poster?)

Yusuf's eyes met his gaze but he couldn't hold it. He looked away immediately, focusing on the pattern etched on his father's wooden desk instead. He felt his throat dry up. He felt paralysed. He couldn't move, couldn't look at his father, and couldn't find the voice to answer him. It was as if all the air from his lungs had been sucked out.

His father walked towards him and stopped right in front of him.

"*Meri gal da jawab woh tu niengan.*" (Answer me. Isn't that you on that poster?)

Lala Ghulam inhaled sharply, a crisp sound shook the air, and then silence. It was as if the world had stopped. There was no more breeze entering the room. It was cold, quiet, and still.

Yusuf finally looked at his father. "Yes," he said, in a quiet voice.

What followed was a loud crack that sent Yusuf's head spinning. The next thing he knew, he was on the floor, his palm on his cheek, rubbing the unmistakable sting of a slap.

"*Nikal ja es khar thu.*" (Get out of this house.)

As Sahab slowly rose to his feet, still shaking from the slap, the beautiful moments he had spent with his father flashed before his eyes. Accompanying him at the local mosque in Peshawar, imitating his strong and proud father, those were just a few of the fond memories that flashed before Yusuf's eyes.

"Will I ever get a chance to spend time with him again? Will my father never love me anymore?" is all young Yusuf could think.

"It was the first time Aghaji had raised his hand on me," Dilip Sahab told me while narrating this incident. "I had never seen him angrier. If it wasn't for Amma and Sakina Aapa, he would've kicked me out of the house that day."

Dilip Sahab smiled to himself.

"Aghaji was a strict disciplinarian and no one dared to speak up against him. But they are just fond memories now. Those were the days."

He was chuckling, but I could tell he was missing his father. The young boy would probably give anything to spend just one more second with his father, the man he looked up to all his life.

"When Aghaji used to get really angry, my mother would save us. My mother's love and father's magnanimity towards us are the reasons our childhood was so happy."

Dilip Sahab's father didn't watch his son's movies for the first two years. Despite living under one roof, they would avoid each other as much as possible. Eventually though, Lala Ghulam warmed up to his son upon the intervention of a dear family friend, Professor Dar of Ismail Yusuf College.

Sahab would often tell me about his fear of Dilip Kumar. The world wanted to meet the legend, and Yusuf, a young, shy man, was scared of the persona he played in front of the world. A private man was now a movie star, but he found it immensely difficult to accept himself the way the world accepted him. It was during this time that Lala Ghulam, the proud Pathan, forced his child out of his shell, to accept and embrace the love he was being given. He would encourage Sahab to meet visitors, media and his fans.

When Dilip Kumar would ask his father why he was required to step out and meet everyone, his father would smile and say, "The branch that bears fruit bends in humility."

8

The Debutant Who Couldn't Run Too Slow

Jwar Bhata did not perform well at the box office. His next two movies also met with only partial success. Dilip Sahab once told me that when he first started out as an actor, he had absolutely no idea what to do. He would skim through the script, assume the personality of the character and behave in the manner he believed the character would behave. I don't know too much about acting but I know Dilip Kumar introduced a new style of acting. If I were to label him as a 'method actor', I can safely say he was the first one in the world. He had no guru or guide. Sahab always told me that whatever few tips he received were from Ashok Kumar and S. Mukherji sahab.

There was a hilarious incident from his first day at a shoot that he narrated to me. We were sitting on his terrace one evening, basking in the sun and enjoying the gentle breeze. A house help had served delicious pakoras, sandwiches and tea for us. The setting was perfect for a story.

"Facing the camera for the first time was unnerving. I was so scared, I felt like running away and never returning," Dilip Sahab said.

It was early morning and the *Jwar Bhata* crew were ready for the shoot. Amiya Chakravarty, the director, had just explained the first shot to everyone.

It was a simple scene. The heroine was upset and would run towards a nearby well to commit suicide. The hero, Dilip Kumar, would run behind her and save her from jumping into the well.

"Once Amiya Chakravarty explained the shot, I imagined how it would go and was ready to shoot," Dilip Sahab said, warming up to the story. "As planned, the actress started running towards the well when the camera started rolling. But instead of me running after her to save her, she was running behind me."

"Cut!" the director bellowed.

Slightly concerned, he walked up to Dilip Kumar and said, "You have to run *behind* the girl, not *ahead* of her."

Sahab voiced his doubt without hesitation. "She runs so slow that I am catching up to her in no time. That's the problem."

Amiya just stared at Dilip Sahab. No one knows what went on his head but he definitely must have cursed his stars for having to work with an actor so green that he couldn't execute a simple scene. The director called the heroine and told her that she had to run faster because Dilip Kumar could not slow down. She just looked at Dilip Sahab, perplexed, and went back to her starting position.

This time, when the director said, "Action!", the heroine ran as fast as she could. Thankfully, she was quick enough so the scene was executed properly.

"I don't think anyone on that set ever forgot that young boy who didn't know how to run slow," Dilip Sahab quipped, and we both burst out laughing. We laughed so much our sides ached. Dilip Sahab gasped for breath and said, "It was my first experience in front of the camera, and what an experience it was." And we started laughing again.

Dilip Sahab always made sure that his acting was congruent with the character and the script. He wanted to give it his all in his performance, so when the audience saw the movie, they felt a genuine connection. That is why Dilip Sahab only worked on one movie at a time.

From the very beginning, Dilip Sahab used to get involved in all aspects of film-making, so much so that people would sometimes get irritated as they perceived his enthusiasm as interference. In the early days, his friend and mentor Ashok Kumar used to tell him, "Stop interfering so much, Yusuf. The producer will get angry and throw you out of the project someday."

That day never came, but his acting improved by leaps and bounds. He went on to become the most celebrated actor in the history of Indian cinema. His acting and knowledge about the world of movies inspired many youngsters to join the industry. His 'interference' was the reason behind some of the biggest box-office successes. With every movie, he learnt something new. It was this constant hunger for knowledge and improvement that helped him outgrow the 'really bad actor' tag he received after his first movie and evolve into the 'legend' he went on to become.

During the 1940s, there were several Urdu and English magazines that catered to movie enthusiasts. One of the most prominent ones was called *Film India*. It was revered by everyone, from the members of the film fraternity to movie buffs. Baburao Patel, the editor, owner and publisher of the monthly magazine, was a prolific reporter with great command over the English language. He used to review films for his magazine. Patel was highly critical as a reviewer and never minced words. His reviews were as admired as they were feared.

Dilip Sahab once quoted Patel's review of *Jwar Bhata* from the 1944 issue of *Film India*. It had read, "My advice to Dilip Kumar is that he should focus his time and energy on eating more food and building some muscle. Maybe build some stamina too. His appearance on screen is a disappointment."

I gawked at Sahab, stunned that he was smiling as he recollected his initial years as an actor. I asked him, "Didn't you find it demoralizing when you read that?"

"I didn't read it. I didn't even know about *Film India*. Baburao had also written a review of my second movie, which did not perform as well as we had expected. Let me just say he wasn't too kind to me in that review as well. Some people who had read them told me about the reviews. That's how I came to know of their existence."

Baburao Patel, after reviewing the first two of Sahab's movies, strongly believed that this young man did not possess any talent, and Bombay Talkies would do themselves a favour if they replaced him with someone with more substance.

After his first two films, however, Dilip Sahab introspected on his style and work and devoted all his energy to improving his performance. He started talking to the lighting guys to understand which angle worked best for him, he would speak to the sound guys for tips on improving his voice clarity, he would speak to the camerapersons to understand how the camera would move in a scene, he would discuss the script at length with the scriptwriter and the director to truly understand the character and the tonality they were aiming for, and he would go the extra length to ensure the chemistry with his co-stars felt genuine. He worked hard and he worked passionately, putting in his heart and soul into his performances and movies.

And the results soon followed. He tasted tremendous success and received appreciation and love from both audience and critics alike. It appeared as if he had found out the 'secret' to making good films.

One evening, while on a stroll at Jogger's Park in Bandra, Sahab told me that secret.

"To make anything successful, there's a lot of teamwork involved. No artist should think that a movie became a success because of their solo effort or their acting. A movie becomes successful because of the entire team's effort, hard work, and a little bit of luck."

If you've ever heard the term 'it takes a village', that's exactly what every project needs. Be it the film industry, a well-established multinational company, or a start-up. That's why Dilip Sahab made friends. He forged lifelong bonds with every person on set and learnt from them through observations and interactions. He would alter his demeanour according to each individual, making them feel comfortable in his presence.

Achievement takes a lot of hard work, and sometimes, even that's not enough. Sometimes, despite everything, there's failure. What then?

True to his nature, Sahab had an answer for that too. He would raise his eyebrows in a very 'intellectual' sort of manner, "No matter how much work you put into something, if it's not meant to be, it's not meant to be. If the audience doesn't like your movie, the audience doesn't like your movie. You can try to improve certain aspects of the movie, maybe hire better actors, write better scripts. But there's only so much you can do. Always remember, you should give your hundred per cent, but if it doesn't work, don't let it hold you back. Every day is a new day, a new adventure. Live that. Don't get stuck in the past."

That's the thing about Dilip Sahab. I don't know if it was his age, or years of experience, or if he was just born with it, he had an uncanny ability to look at things exactly the way they were. Simple and uncomplicated. It was such a straightforward statement – if it doesn't work out, it's okay. Move on. Try again. Find something else. Just don't get stuck. Don't get held back because one incident affected you.

"No artist should worry about success. It's written even in the Bhagavad Gita, 'Karam karo, phal ki chinta mat karo' (Keep doing your work, don't worry about the outcome). Make your movie. Do your job. Make the movie a part of who you are. Live the character. Acting is all about not acting."

Dilip Sahab was offered diverse roles and unique characters to play. He used to get completely immersed in these characters. "Every time I played a character, I tried to relate to the character based on my experience. I emulated the emotions from what I've already seen or have gone through or imagine how it would be if it was my real-life," he had told me once.

Sometimes immersing in the character had a downside to it. Dilip Kumar and renowned actress Madhubala had ended their relationship on a sour note and were barely talking on the sets of *Mughal-E-Azam*. They were shooting the scene that leads to the song '*Pyaar Kiya Toh Darna Kya*'. Salim (Dilip Kumar) was made to believe that his lover Anarkali (Madhubala) had betrayed his trust. The scene involved an angry Salim confronting her and slapping her for betraying him.

Madhubala had a serious heart condition that caused her to remain unwell on the sets. She had bouts of fever and weakness and was having a tough time shooting. But when shooting a scene, it was impossible to tell that she was struggling.

The scene was being shot in an exquisite set, a hall of mirrors and that added a surreal beauty to the scene.

The cameras started rolling and Salim, the distraught lover, walked into the room, ready to confront Anarkali. The entire set watched with bated breath.

"*Akbar ki buzdil laundi, tu Salim ki mehbooba nahin. Tu ek jhooti kasam thi jo mera imaan badal gayi. Tu ek sharmnaak badnaami ka woh daag thi jo mere daaman par laga aur dhul gayi.*" (You coward, you're not Salim's lover. You were a false promise that changed my faith. You are a shameful humiliation that stained my clothes and cleansed itself.)

And then came the part where Dilip Kumar slapped Madhubala.

The sharp crack of the slap echoed in the hall of mirrors. Everyone stared for what seemed like an eternity, and then rushed to where Madhubala lay. Her ill health, Dilip Sahab's intensity and the slap had left her stunned. She lay there in her costume, motionless for a few seconds.

The scene was never shot again. There were no retakes. However, a flash of the scene still remains on the reel.

Dilip Sahab felt the pain the character was going through. Unfortunately, the parallels between the movie and real life were too obvious. A man who feels betrayed by his beloved because she favours the parent. Out of respect, I never asked him about it directly, but I believe in that moment, his real emotions surfaced and he could not hold back.

Dilip Sahab always maintained that when he picked roles and movies, he immersed himself into them completely. It was almost like an extension of his own personality. He went so deep into the characters' mind that during the 1950s, he had to battle depression.

Many of the characters played by Dilip Sahab were tormented souls. He was labelled 'Tragedy King', and people expected his movies to be despairing. He used to delve so deep into the character's mind that during the 1950s, there was a period when he was battling depression.

"I was forlorn. Day in and day out, I was in the minds of characters who were lonely, gloomy, on the verge of death, or had lost a lover. That took a toll on me. I had forgotten what it was like to live a happy life. Apart from work, and work-related commitments, I wouldn't step out of my home. I was trying to find joy, but I just couldn't. I was labelled Tragedy King at the young age of twenty-six, when most actors would have wanted such a label after decades of work."

To deal with his depression, he consulted a couple of doctors in London. The team of professional doctors did not know him as an actor, or a social symbol. To them, Dilip Kumar was just a man battling depression, looking for help. Dilip Sahab had opened up to them about his work and his personal life.

"I was scared. I had never before been to a doctor for my emotional well-being. In those times, it was thought that if you visit a psychiatrist, it meant you were crazy. It wasn't an accepted concept. It was looked down upon. I had to leave the country to seek help."

I asked, "How was it, Sahab? What did the experts prescribe?"

"Happiness," was his terse reply.

I was confused. Wasn't the doctor supposed to prescribe medicines to help him reach a state of happiness?

"I'm sorry, Sahab, I don't understand."

"They didn't give me any medication or ask me to do any tests. They concluded just one thing – that my state of mind was a result of the movies I did. My mind would get involved with the character to the point that I would forget his tragedy was his, not mine. I let the tragedy seep into my own life. All I had to do was choose happier movies, comedies and action. I had to stay positive, and surround myself with positivity."

"That sounds too simple."

"It was. It was as simple as it sounds."

Audiences and industry professionals have always tried to label Dilip Sahab's style of acting. Some called him the 'ultimate actor', while others believed him to be the 'best method actor there ever was'. Every person who met him, watched his work, or studied his acting, had a label for his acting. Few people know that Dilip Sahab did not enjoy being labelled. When I asked him about it, Sahab told me that he did not believe in terms like 'method acting', nor did he ascribe to any school of acting.

"Sahab, people have all sorts of labels for your acting style. How would you like to describe your style of acting?"

Although he had probably been asked the same question a million times, he did not look annoyed or irritated. On the contrary, there was a smile on his face. He was always a gentleman.

"There is no 'Dilip Kumar style of acting'. I am just a natural actor. To do justice to the character I am playing, I get into the character's head, understand his personality, and then analyse how he would react or respond in the situations mentioned in the script."

"Sahab, wasn't it difficult to imagine so many situations?"

"It takes practice. Initially I would use experiences from my personal life to try and understand how my character would react. Eventually, I moved to studying the scripts in depth. Understanding the character and his background gave me more insight into how the character would react. I started reading more. I would read the classics and imagine myself in the character's shoes. If there is one thing I have learnt about acting, it is that to truly embrace your character, you have to discard your way of acting. You have to forget about yourself, and truly embody the character you're playing."

"And what would you say to the people who say they should learn by watching your movies and acting techniques?"

Dilip Sahab smiled and turned to me. "If someone says learn from Dilip Kumar, tell them Dilip Kumar is still learning."

There were two things I learnt that day.

First, we must make our work our life, and second, whatever we do, we have to do it with all our heart. We don't need to worry about the outcome. Thousands of inspirational quotes say the same thing. But it is by observing Dilip Sahab that I understood its true meaning. It is not that we must give up our lives for our work. Anything extreme is harmful, so we must strike a balance.

When your work is a task, it slows you down. When your work is your dream, the passion and willingness flow effortlessly. It is this passion that allows you to take risks, and do what needs to be done. A man who loves his work never comes back home unsatisfied. Choose a path that inspires you. Find your inspiration wherever you can, and don't think about whether or not it makes sense. Just start. Do what you have to. Eventually, your idea will take a beautiful shape and make sense to everyone around you.

When I first started my company, I wanted to bring about a change. It was the time when the Internet was booming. I had the opportunity to give people a voice, a platform, where they could speak up about the issues that bothered them. Brands, sellers and dealers had the luxury to sell products without being answerable to their customers. MouthShut was to be the platform where they were answerable.

I believed in my company. I believed in the good it would do for people. It was inspirational to me. With my heart and soul invested, work didn't seem like 'work' anymore. Every morning I woke up, I was looking forward to the day ahead and not dreading it.

Dilip Sahab's work speaks for itself. He worked hard at his job, without worrying about becoming a star. He did his part, and the rewards followed.

9

One from the Fans: A Creation of God

In 2003, I happened to run into a Dilip Kumar fan. He came to my office during a particularly languid afternoon. At first glance I could tell he was not from Mumbai. He was tall, well-built, had thick black hair that casually framed his face. His suit was dark blue, with just enough glimmer to let me know that it was expensive. His shirt looked slightly crumpled, as if he had been out all day. He had a look of determination on his face.

I met him in my cabin. As he entered, I offered my hand as a greeting. His grip was firm and short. Every inch of him screamed money. I wondered what brought him to my workplace.

As he introduced himself, my curiosity increased. I didn't waste time and called the staff to bring us some tea and snacks.

He looked comfortable sitting in the faux leather chair across the table. After a few minutes of small talk, he abruptly said, "I want to meet Dilip Kumar."

His request threw me off balance. I had never encountered such a request before, and was certainly not prepared to answer it. I was visibly uncomfortable. The man continued to study me with a smile on his face. His smile was pleading, with a hint of arrogance that often comes with affluence.

In his baritone, he continued, "I have been trying to meet Dilip Kumar for long now. I have tried calling, writing, even sent a fax. I have not received a response."

I smiled. I thought to myself: another one of Dilip Kumar's fans.

"Why do you think I will be able to help you? Sir, I'm glad you reached out to me, but I don't believe I'll be able to help you in this matter."

"Why not?"

"You're asking me to introduce you to Dilip Kumar. He is Dilip Kumar, and only he can authorize who he meets. I could mention it to him, but I cannot take you to meet him."

But he persisted. He started telling me about his accomplishments and his ostentatious clout, trying to convince me to take him to Dilip Kumar.

After he was done, I simply said, "I'm sorry but that's not possible. In any case, Sahab is out of town. I'm sorry you had to come all the way."

His face fell. He looked disappointed. We decided to remain in touch, a general courtesy you offer anyone you meet. Finally, he left but not without yet another appeal to get him a meeting with Dilip Kumar. Never before had a man walked into my office so consumed with the need to meet Dilip Kumar.

The next day, to my shock, horror, and slight amusement, the man returned to my office. Today he was wearing a lighter shade than the day before. A light-blue suit hung effortlessly on his broad shoulders.

I received him at the reception desk. "Hello, Faisal," he greeted.

Trying to compose myself, I replied, "Hello. What a surprise."

"You can hardly call this a surprise. I thought since I didn't ask you when Sahab would be back from his trip, let me meet you again and give it another try."

I could hardly believe what I was hearing. "Sahab is not back yet. I don't know when he will be back."

"Oh, how is that possible. I don't believe it. I'm sure you know of his travel plans. After all, you are so close to him."

I was suddenly interested in this man. I had assumed that he had befriended somebody common and found me.

"How did you find out about our friendship?"

"I asked around about how I could get a meeting with Dilip Kumar and someone told me about you being close to him."

Meeting Dilip Kumar was a task in itself. He had a humble office on the ground floor of his bungalow with staff and a secretary who handled all of his communication. There would be at least a hundred phone calls every day, and even more letters, and fax messages. Getting through them all was laborious.

"Look, I just want to meet him for ten minutes," he continued. "I know everyone talks about Dilip Sahab and says they're his fans, but I'm not just a fan. I worship that man. He is my god."

I had to stop myself from falling off my chair. With a stern face, I had to let him know his request was impossible to grant. When I bid the man goodbye, I wasn't sure whether to be amazed at him, or feel sad for him.

A few days later, Sahab returned from his trip. I was at my office, busy with some work, when my receptionist transferred a call on my landline.

"Faisal Sahab, please hold the line, Dilip Sahab wants to speak to you."

It was Dilip Sahab's secretary on the other end. I waited patiently as he handed the phone to Sahab. After a slight shuffling sound, I heard Sahab.

"How are you?"

His warm and energetic voice always brought a smile to my face.

"By God's grace. I'm well, Sahab. How are you? How was your trip?"

"Yes, it was pretty good. Where are you now?"

"Sahab, I'm at the office."

"All right, come home after work. We will go to Jogger's Park together. Do one thing, come at 7 p.m."

"Yes, absolutely. I will be there at 7 p.m."

As promised, I was at Dilip Sahab's home promptly by 7 p.m. My driver dropped me off at the porch of his bungalow and I made my way inside the house. I walked straight towards the lift. As I stood there waiting for the lift to reach the second floor, the smell of freshly prepared snacks wafted towards me. Saira baji had arranged for some hot snacks for all of us on the terrace.

When I reached the second floor, my muscle memory prompted me to walk towards the comfortable couch at the far end of the living room. Sahab was ready. He was wearing his white kurta and pyjama bottoms, and had a beige shawl wrapped around him. On his feet, he wore his comfortable walking shoes.

"Assalama'alaikum, Sahab."

He turned around and smiled. His eyes crinkled on the sides and I knew he was as happy to see me as I was to see him.

"Walaikumsalam. Come sit. Eat something before we go for our walk."

I walked up to him, hugged him, and sat right beside him.

"What will you have, Sahab?"

A house help was trying to serve us snacks, when Sahab asked him to let me arrange his plate.

I extended my arms to reach up to the low coffee table in front of us. There were quite a few delicacies. I picked up two plates and filled them with samosas, sandwiches, and a few other snacks. I added the sauces on the side of the plate, and then turned towards Sahab. He gingerly took the plate from my hands, and insisted that he would first feed the samosa to me.

I retorted, "Sahab, I have a plate ready for me too. This one's for you."

"You've set my plate up and served it to me, so I will feed you from my plate first."

It was his innocent way of saying thank you. For me it was an honour to serve him but he made it an honour to feed me with his hands.

At about 8 p.m., we were ready to leave for Jogger's Park. Dilip Sahab informed Saira baji, who came out to see him off. Even after years of their marriage, their love was no less than a budding romance between two teenagers. They were adorable. She walked up to him, adjusted his shawl, fussed over him a little, looked at me sharply and reminded me that he needed his walk, and headed indoors only after our cars had exited the property.

Dilip Sahab looked at her as she headed towards the door. He had that look in his eyes that told you that their love had not dwindled over the years. In fact, it may have grown.

A few minutes later, we reached Jogger's Park. As Sahab walked in, most of the people walking stopped and turned around to stare at the legend. Some walked up to him to say hello, some requested for autographs, and some continued to look at him from afar.

Sahab politely obliged the sparse crowd, and then gracefully bid them goodbye. A few of them were instructed to leave by the two security guards around him.

After about five rounds, we sat down at a bench overlooking the sea.

"Sahab, do you know who came to my office a few days ago?" I asked eagerly, as I was dying to tell him the story.

Sahab, slightly curious, asked me, "Who?"

I told Sahab how the man had come to my office, asking me to set up a meeting with him. I told him how he had persisted despite me telling him I could not help him.

"The man said to me that he was not just your fan. He worships you. All his life, he's had only one wish: to meet you, even if for a moment. He worships you to the point that he never utters your name unless he's made *wudu* (the Muslim ritual washing before namaz). He only utters your name after he's made wudu."

Dilip Sahab snapped his head towards me. He could not believe what he heard.

"May Allah forgive him and forgive me. That innocent man does not know what he has said."

Dilip Sahab was shocked. Comparing him to a god was borderline blasphemy. His face had a shadow of disappointment and sadness.

After a pause, he looked towards the horizon, and spoke aloud, "*Tera khayal hai, tera jamaal hai, tu hai. Mujhe ye tabish-o-danish kahan ki main kya hoon.*" (It's your thought, it's your beauty, it's you. I have no idea what I am.)

His words, and his silence, spoke legions about him. It's not that he wasn't aware of how people perceived him. He was. He had always seen people hang on to every word he uttered, he had noticed the sudden silence when he walked into a room, but he never allowed it to get the better of him.

He never took pride in the affection he received. He accepted it with humility and respect. Dilip Sahab considered himself a hard-working man and not a 'star' as everyone else saw him as. Acting was his work. Dilip Kumar was his work. Yusuf was not Dilip Kumar. Yusuf never became bigger than Dilip Kumar.

He'd say this to me all the time. And then he'd smile. That was his little way of keeping himself grounded.

Having enjoyed his company for so many years, I knew exactly how much people loved him. It was an incident in 1998 that first brought this to my attention.

It was August and I was in Mumbai for my summer break. I was studying in New York back then, and had come down to visit my family after the final exams. I was due to return to the US in a week. While I was in the city, my brother Asif informed me that Sahab had been enquiring about me and that I should go and meet him.

I was quite young back then and didn't interact with Sahab as often as I should have. I was busy with college, and in hindsight, spending time with Dilip Sahab was not even on my radar. Although I had the utmost respect for him, I didn't think of him as dearly as I do now. Asif was the closest to him among all family members, but since Sahab had specifically asked about me, I wanted to go and meet him at the earliest.

Since Dilip Sahab's house was a mere ten minutes away from mine, I decided to walk. When I reached, Asif bhai was already engrossed in a deep conversation with Sahab. He looked up at me as I walked in and, with a beaming smile, informed Sahab that I had arrived.

Sahab called me close and we exchanged greetings. After the initial five minutes of small talk, Sahab paused and asked, "How've you been? What's keeping you busy these days?"

Even before I could hang my head in shame for not meeting him more frequently in the long summer break, Sahab smiled and asked, "Would you like to accompany us to Kuwait?"

My face lit up and my heart jumped with joy.

"Yes, absolutely. It will be an honour to travel with you."

"Asif is also coming with us. It'll be great if you came too."

I smiled in agreement and said I couldn't wait to accompany him on a trip.

"Okay then. Start packing your bags soon."

"By the way, Sahab, when are we going?"

"In two to three days."

I was thrown off-balance. When Dilip Sahab, in his love and grace, asked me to accompany him on a trip, I assumed he was planning a holiday of sorts in advance. I imagined there'd be months to plan the holiday dates, pack my essentials, and get ahead of the workload, if there was any. I was mentally preparing that this trip would be in four to six months, just in time for my college winter or spring break. Two to three days seemed too short a time to plan an international trip.

Dilip Sahab had been invited by the Indian ambassador in Kuwait, B.M.C. Nair, to grace the Indians in Kuwait with his presence at the Indian Independence Day celebrations. It would be an official trip and he would be the chief guest at the event. They had scheduled for him to attend the main event on 15 August, meet dignitaries, citizens, lawmakers and the ruler of Kuwait. Also arranged were a few interviews with distinguished publications and TV channels of the country.

"But, Sahab, I won't be able to make it. My college begins soon, and I have to return to New York in a week."

My heart was racing as I was not sure of the choice of my words in declining the first-ever offer to travel with Dilip Kumar.

There was a long pause. The room was quiet. I could hear my own heartbeat and the sound of the air-conditioner seemed louder than it was a moment ago. I looked at his face and he smiled at me.

"Well then, we shall travel with you some other time."

I was disheartened, but there would be other chances. He promised me a trip with him. He would accompany me one day. In all the years I knew Dilip Sahab, every word he had uttered only made others around him feel more important. His choice of words always raised my spirits. He could have said you'll have another chance to travel with me, but he chose to honour me instead. He was magnanimous. Both statements held the possibility of travel with Dilip Sahab, the only difference was that one statement made him important, and the other, me. I smiled, and the evening continued with Asif bhai and Dilip Sahab planning their Kuwait trip.

They were scheduled to take an early-morning Kuwait Airways flight on 14 August. In the 1990s, it was mandatory for international passengers to reach the airport a minimum of two-and-a-half hours prior to boarding, which meant they had to be at the airport no later than 3.30 a.m.

At around 2.30 a.m., I decided to accompany them to the airport.

"Okay, let's go. First, we have to go to Dilip Sahab's house. From there we will head to the airport together," Asif bhai told me.

When we reached Sahab's home, he was ready with his luggage in the car's trunk. We stepped out of our car to greet him, and Sahab noticed that I was driving.

"You didn't get the driver along?"

"It's quite late at night. So, I thought I would drive the car and see you off at the airport."

"Okay then, I will come in your car with you. You follow my car."

As we approached the departure gate, I could see a huge crowd waiting for Dilip Sahab to arrive. The crowd seemed like a swarm of bees, the buzz audible from far away. Sahab's car carefully snaked its way past security into the human wave. It slowed down and eventually came to a halt. I could hardly see the sedan, but when it stopped, the security immediately formed a tight circle around the vehicle, preventing any unauthorized personnel from coming close to it.

Dilip Sahab was heading to Kuwait for an official event and the security matched the gravitas. Unfortunately for the crowd, Dilip Sahab wasn't in that car. One man stepped away from the cadre and approached Sahab's car. With a leader-like charisma, he opened the door and seemed slightly surprised that there was no one inside except the driver. Being a high-ranking official, he didn't let his surprise linger for long. The driver probably explained the situation to him because he soon shut the car door and looked in our direction.

The officer spoke to his men and without missing a beat, they had our car covered. He then proceeded to open the car door to allow Dilip Sahab to exit. The moment people realized that Dilip Kumar was in the other car, they were pulsating against the human barricade created by the security guards.

Asif Bhai seemed unperturbed, but I was having a hard time imagining us walk past the crowd. At one point, I was scared for our lives. The security was exceptional, and despite my trepidation, we reached the airport entrance safely.

I was walking behind Dilip Sahab and Asif bhai. As soon as we reached the gate, I called out to my brother to wish him goodbye. Sahab heard my farewell and turned around.

"You will leave from here? Please come inside."

Sahab looked at the security personnel beside him, and confirmed that his assistant had in fact secured a visitor's pass for me so I could enter the airport building without hiccups. The security personnel spoke on his walkie-talkie, turned towards me, and with a slight smile, asked me to enter the airport with them.

The walkway from the main entrance to immigration, the point till which I could accompany Sahab and Asif bhai, was about three minutes, but it took us more than fifteen. There were scores of people, passengers and airport staff, waiting to shake Dilip Kumar's hand. They all wanted to say hello, and Sahab humoured them all.

When we reached the immigration area, it was finally time to bid adieu. I hugged my elder brother and wished him a safe journey. I then hugged Sahab lightly and wished him the same. Sahab held my hand and asked me if I needed assistance returning to the car.

"It won't be a problem, you please don't worry," I assured him. He refused to accept it. Sahab turned to the same security personnel and requested, "Can you please escort our guest till the exit. Can I entrust him to your security?"

I was touched by his gesture. I finally bid them both goodbye and proceeded to head to my car.

Two airport security personnel were with me throughout. When we reached the gate, I could see the crowd still pulsating outside. This time though, I was not nervous. I was alone, a simple man, heading back to my car. Obviously, I was mistaken.

As soon as I stepped out into the crowd, I got mobbed. People of all ages and sizes tried to make their way to me. At first, I was shocked, unable to understand what was happening. I was hoping and praying that the security personnel would be able to get me away from the mob.

The closer I got to the car, the more I started noticing what people were doing. They were grabbing my hand and trying to kiss it. A woman, tears running down her cheeks, exclaimed, "I had one wish in this life: to see Dilip Kumar in person someday. Today my eyes have found peace."

One man, seemingly in his early thirties, gripped my hand tight and started crying. He planted kisses on my hands as tears rolled down his face, his quivering voice exclaiming, "My dream has come true today. The hand that touched Dilip Kumar is the hand I am touching."

I was shocked. People were only excited by the prospect of holding the hand that held Dilip Kumar's hands!

That was the day I realized how much Dilip Sahab was truly loved and cherished by everyone. Dilip Kumar was not just an actor, not just another man to them.

"He was the reason they all woke up in the morning," as Lord Meghnad Desai wrote in his book *Nehru's Hero: Dilip Kumar in the Life of India*. He was the one creation of God that could not be easily compared to anyone else.

Having never been a keen lover of movies, I had only heard of his fame as an actor who was apparently the biggest icon anyone had ever seen, but I felt the true impact of his stardom that morning at the airport.

Making our way through the crowd and the commotion, I don't think I will ever forget the fear I felt that day. It is etched in my memory for life. As I stepped out of the airport terminal, I heard one of the security personnel say, "What a creation of God Dilip Kumar is."

10

Paying It Forward,
the Dilip Sahab Way

There were only a select few places Dilip Sahab and I met. Sometimes we met at his house, or we went for a drive. Other times, we used to meet at Taj Land's End for a cup of tea or coffee, or stroll at Jogger's Park.

I enjoyed the times spent with him at Jogger's Park the most. We would usually meet at around 9 p.m. and walk for about forty-five minutes, after which we would find a bench to sit and just talk. It was a different bench each time. Sometimes we would sit by the sea, and other times, we would sit by the small pond.

When it was time for us to leave, Sahab always insisted on dropping me home, although I had my own car. "Ask your driver to follow us in your car," he used to say.

Jogger's Park has been a popular haunt since its establishment in 1990. Thousands of people in and around Bandra flock to the park every day. Some come there and

At an event I accompanied him, 2004.

Office visit. Dilip Kumar in my chair, 2005.

Amitabh Bachchan, Jaya Bachchan, Abhishek Bachchan at Dilip Kumar's 89th birthday celebration, 2011.

Within a few days of opening his Twitter account, he gained 100,000 followers, 2011.

At a small family get-together to celebrate the Padma Vibhushan. Seated next to him is his youngest brother Ahsan Khan. Next to me is Saira Banu and my wife Aabeda, 2016.

Receiving the Padma Vibhushan, India's second-highest civilian award from the then Home Minister, Rajnath Singh, and Governor of Maharashtra, Vidyasagar Rao, 2015.

In Medina, Hotel Oberoi, after Zohar prayers, 2013.

Leaving Medina for Makkah. Wearing the simple white ihram, a state of mental and physical purity, 2013.

Spirituallly thrilled after Umrah, Dilip Kumar extends Makkah stay

SIRAJ WAHAB
ARAB NEWS STAFF

Legendary Indian actor Muhammad Yousuf Khan — who attained world fame with his screen name Dilip Kumar — and his actress wife Saira Bano have been so touched and spiritually exhilarated by their journey to Makkah that they have extended their stay in the holy city by a couple of more days.

"Dilip Kumar performed Umrah along with a 21-member entourage three days ago ... He was absolutely thrilled and spiritually charged," said Faisal I. Farooqui, a close family friend and CEO of mouthshut.com.

Farooqui tweeted about the thespian's visit to Makkah and Madinah and posted interesting pictures on Twitter account (@FaisalMouthshut).

Talking to Arab News yesterday, Farooqui said one of the most poignant moments during the journey was when Dilip Kumar was performing the circumambulation of the Holy Kaaba.

"He was full of energy and was reading aloud verses from the Holy Qur'an while performing the 'tawaf.' When we all heard him speak aloud, we started repeating the prayers after him," said a very excited Farooqui. "Those were very touching moments, especially because Sahib is a man of few words."

During the circumambulation, Dilip Kumar was in total awe. "He was involved in all aspects of the religious rituals ... whether it was the donning of the ihram in Madinah, or performing the 'tawaf' or saee in Makkah, he was a picture of total submission to Almighty Allah. He was fully engrossed," said Farooqui. "I have not seen him in a more composed and serene manner in such a long time."

A cool and composed Dilip Kumar in ihram on his way to perform Umrah. (AN photos by Faisal Farooqui)

Farooqui said two people should find special mention while writing about Dilip Kumar's journey to the holy land. "They are Saira Banu and her brother Sultan Ahmad. Without Saira Baji's extraordinary energy and Sultan Bhai and his family's support, the whole trip would not have been possible," he said.

He said "Sahib and Saira Baji" were touched by the generosity extended by everyone during their stay in Madinah and Makkah. "All of them were gracious and polite. They understood the family's concern for Sahib's well-being and were very supportive. The people in

Dilip Kumar with close family friend Faisal Farooqui after performing Umrah.

Madinah ... the people in Makkah ... they were all very, very helpful," Farooqui, whose family has been friendly with Dilip Kumar for the last 50 years, said the legendary actor and his entourage were to leave for Mumbai last evening. "But such has been the impact of the journey on them that they decided to extend their stay in the holy city," he said. "No one feels like leaving Makkah."

Indian Consul General Faiz Ahmad Kidwai met them at the Makkah Hilton on Thursday evening and said one could clearly see happiness on Dilip Kumar's face. "He speaks very little, but one could easily read his radiant face; he seemed contented."

During their conversation with the consul general, they expressed their interest of coming back to the Kingdom soon. "Dilip Kumar and Saira Banu intend to perform Haj this year. This is their intention and we all should pray for their dream to come true," said Kidwai. "Saira Banu said they don't feel like leaving Makkah and that is the reason why they have extended their stay."

Kidwai kept his men in Makkah on standby for any possible help. "This is their private visit, but it was our duty to

extend all help to this great symbol of our country," he said.

Farooqui echoed the consul general's sentiments. "Let us all pray that they come back to the holy land. We all are truly blessed to accompany them to Makkah and Madinah." The entourage included eight of Dilip Kumar's longtime support staff, including his personal doctor and a cook.

Born on Dec. 11, 1922, in Peshawar, Yousuf Khan joined the film industry in 1944. He is rightly considered as the Subcontinent's first method actor and an inspiration for generations of filmstars.

Yousuf Khan has been an inspiration behind many generations of actors. His dialogue delivery, flawless Urdu and acting abilities have all endeared him to his fellow actors and fans. In his days, he was the king of Indian film industry and his dialogues in the film "Mughal-e-Azam" — a true love epic — was on the lips of every moviegoer and literature lover. In one of his famous observations, noted film director Mahesh Bhatt said "Where would Indian cinema be without Dilip Kumar's heart-wrenching performances in Mughal-e-Azam? The wells from where we drink water were dug by this giant called Dilip Kumar."

Umrah trip headline news in Saudi Arabia's largest English newspaper Arab News. Dilip Kumar asked me to give the interview on his behalf, 2013.

Lata Mangeshkar visited him after hearing about his brief illness in 2015.

Wedding picture. Dilip Kumar and Saira Banu, October 1966.

Wedding picture. Dilip Kumar and Saira Banu, October 1966. Naseem Banu, Saira Banu's mother, to her right.

workout, some to meet their friends and most people just come for their morning and evening walks.

Prior to 1990, the land where Jogger's Park is now situated was a garbage dump where all of Bandra's waste was dumped.

Oliver Andrade, a local hockey and football coach from the nearby St Stanislaus High School, came up with the idea of transforming the stinky dump into a park. During the 1980s, the Bombay Municipal Corporation (BMC) had created opportunities for local bodies to claim unused lands and dump yards and create public utility spaces. So, Coach Oliver approached Dilip Sahab with his plans.

Dilip Sahab supported the idea and used every resource available to him to help achieve Oliver Andrade's dream. That's why when he requested to keep the park open after 9 p.m. for his sake, they had obliged. It's not that Sahab wanted extra favours because he had helped set up the park. The problem was that when he used to step out, he was flocked by people looking for autographs, pictures or a conversation. Not only was it an inconvenience to him and the people accompanying him, but also to the others at the park who wanted to go about their activities peacefully. So, Sahab, followed by his security personnel, used to go for a walk after the park shut its gates to the general public.

One day, it was after 10 p.m. and we were sitting on one of the sea-facing benches, enjoying the strong breeze. There was a soft yellow glow around us from the streetlight above, and complete darkness beyond. It was calm, eerie and beautiful. It was just us, the wind and the sound of the waves crashing against the rocks.

His voice cut through the air, "The park looks so beautiful now. Oliver Andrade's hard work has paid off."

That day, Sahab told me about the day Oliver Andrade had approached him with his plan. It was a warm afternoon, and he, like everyone else, had taken an appointment to meet Sahab at his home office. He had reached on time, dressed in his Sunday best.

As Sahab descended the stairs to meet Oliver, the coach had stood up immediately, and with a straight back and broad shoulders, walked up to greet him.

Sahab had been happy to see Coach Oliver. He was aware of his contributions to the society and his skills as a coach. A football enthusiast himself, Sahab had very high regard for sports coaches.

"Dilip Sahab, as you know, BMC is using the land next to Otter's Club as a garbage dump. It's right by the sea, and such an eyesore. That entire area stinks to high heavens. It's also harmful for the environment," Oliver had said.

"I agree. But what are you planning to do about it?"

"Sahab, I want to create a beautiful park, with lawns and trees and flower gardens. I want it to be a place where people can come to appreciate the greenery and the seaside, sit, have a peaceful time."

Dilip Sahab was the co-founder and president of the Otter's Club, an elite club that everybody wanted to be a part of. Otter's Club promoted sports, focusing on swimming and squash. It has even produced some fine athletes. Being a sports zealot, Sahab was the obvious choice to approach for assistance and support.

He heard Oliver Andrade's idea and said, "That sounds interesting. However, why not build a place that could help the children and youth bloom."

"I'm sorry I don't understand."

There was a piece of paper in front of Sahab. He picked it up and placed it on the table between Oliver and him. He grabbed a pen from his front pocket and drew four straight lines on the paper, and then pushed it towards Oliver Andrade.

"Here, why don't you try to also include some jogging tracks to your plan? People will love it and they will also benefit greatly when it finally opens up to the public."

"You're right, Sahab. It is a wonderful suggestion. I will work on the plans immediately."

As Oliver Andrade left, Dilip Sahab's excitement increased. He was to be a part of a project that was going to change the face of Bandra forever.

Slowly, but surely, the plan emerged into a full-scale blueprint, and Sahab and Oliver Andrade started bringing the park to life. Their first step was to get permission from the authorities. Having been involved in political campaigns, and as former sheriff of Bombay, Dilip Sahab had little trouble getting in touch with the right people.

Once he got them on the phone, all he had to do was nudge a bit. He spoke and met with the senior leadership in the Maharashtra government and used his personal connections to secure permissions required to go ahead with the project.

"You must've worked hard on this project," I told Dilip Sahab, as we continued talking in the warm yellow glow on that seaside bench.

"Oliver Andrade was always there, front and centre. I was so happy to see a member of the community work hard to create something so beautiful for the people. He did everything from preparing the blueprint and estimates to overseeing the progress. All I did was help him achieve his dream."

I smiled at Dilip Sahab. It was such a typical reaction. Sahab never bragged and he was always humble. I wonder how many other projects he had undertaken, but never even talked about – for instance, his foundational role in the setting up of a Film City in Mumbai. He had all the fame and money one could want. He had luxuries I dared not imagine, and his heart was as pure as could be.

"Next, we had to arrange funds or sponsors for the execution of the project. And that was going to be a task, because Oliver Andrade didn't have money. It was our duty to start talking to people and getting them to donate their time and money."

Dilip Sahab and Oliver Andrade started planning the way forward. They approached Dilip Sahab's close friend, Sunil Dutt, who was then the sheriff of Bombay and a Member of Parliament, in addition to being a resident of Pali Hill, Bandra. Sunil Dutt offered his assistance in completing the project.

Dilip Kumar then approached Siraj Lokhandwala, a popular and respected name in the world of real estate and construction. He had made his fortune in the late 1970s and '80s by developing a huge tract of marshy land in North Mumbai, close to the Andheri-Versova area. Mr Lokhandwala's hard work and entrepreneurial acumen led to the development of an entire township. Today, Lokhandwala Complex boasts of some of Mumbai's most upmarket apartments, home to movie stars and actors of every hue, and houses some of the most famous retail brands. Siraj Lokhandwala was a big fan and a friend of Dilip Sahab.

"When the time came to find funds and builders for the construction of the park, only one name came to my mind. Siraj. I always found him to be a very hard-working man, and a decent human being."

That Siraj Lokhandwala was pleasantly shocked when Dilip Kumar approached him would probably be an understatement. Dilip Kumar had personally asked Siraj to help. But he was a smart businessman too. I suppose he believed that his contribution to the new park in Bandra would gain him goodwill and earn him the respect that usually does not come easily to construction company owners. And so, the Lokhandwala builders were on board. They would construct the entire park, that too from their own private funds.

If anyone has ever been to Jogger's Park, they know the importance of the boundary wall abutting the Arabian Sea. The heavily fortified high wall on three sides is the one thing that separates the park from the water, especially during high tides. Oliver Andrade, with Dilip Sahab's help, approached the famous Raheja Builders and Rizvi Builders for the construction of the boundary wall. Both the builders were more than happy to contribute their time and resources for the job. And thus, the park's construction started.

"It was a joy to watch everything come to life bit by bit. They created the jogging track, the tiled path for walks, a small pond in the middle, complete with ducks and fishes. That small bridge above it made the pond even more romantic. My favourite part of the park is the playground in the middle. All the swings and slides, and watching the children scream and shout with glee. It is Bandra's very own heaven."

Jogger's Park, the first of its kind in India, was opened to the public on 27 May 1990. There was, however, no one to maintain it. Jogger's Park was built on BMC-owned land, but the corporation did not have the resources to maintain the park. Dilip Sahab once again reached out to Siraj Lokhandwala and asked him if he could take the ownership of the park's maintenance. He agreed. And thus, under the Lokhandwala Builders Group, the Bombay Suburban Civic Trust was created. They gained rights from the BMC to take care of the maintenance and upkeep of the park.

After Oliver Andrade's demise, a small plaque was put up at the park's entrance. It says 'From Sir, With Love'.

Apart from Jogger's Park, Dilip Sahab had involved himself in innumerable other causes over the years. His association and mammoth contribution in the forming of the National Association for the Blind (NAB) is no secret. His role in the movie *Deedar* introduced audiences to the struggles of the blind. Sahab, along with Veera Rao, campaigned and raised money for the construction of the NAB, which has impacted hundreds of thousands of people's lives.

This streak of reaching out to the community stretched way back to the partition which had a huge impact on millions of families, including Dilip Kumar's. "We were so shaken after the massive losses we had to endure. Then there were stories about the lives lost and the struggles everyone faced. It was too much to bear."

Dilip Sahab knew he had to do something to help the people moving to and from India. He travelled to the capital, Delhi, and urged the government, insisting they help people by raising money to provide jobs and shelter to those who now found themselves refugees. Sahab helped set up countless rehabs to assist the people who were resettling.

"Sahab, do you remember the days of the partition?"

"There are very few events in life which change the course of history. The Partition was one of them," he said.

I had waited for him to continue, but he had not. In all my years of knowing him, he never spoke much about the Partition. When the Partition was announced, Sahab had already started his acting career but was not a superstar yet. It was only in 1947, with his movie *Jugnu*, that he became a star. I used to see the pain reflected in his eyes in his refusal to speak about the Partition. I believe it could have been why Dilip Sahab was so considerate and involved in helping people. He had seen enough hatred to realize that what the world needed was love and compassion.

Recently, I visited a dermatologist. On the wall behind the doctor's chair was a photograph. I leaned forward a bit for a clearer look at the photo and recognized the kind face of the man I love dearly. In the photo, Dilip Sahab was standing behind a bright red ribbon, dressed to the nines, a pair of shiny scissors in his hand, with the beaming doctor beside him.

"Dilip Sahab inaugurated your clinic?"

"All I did was somehow manage to reach him personally and invite him. He accepted, but did not promise. A few days later, I left a message with his secretary and received confirmation that he will come. My family and friends were so happy and shocked to see him. He truly is a man of his words."

Dilip Sahab always turned up. If he said he would, he did. He attended openings, functions, weddings and any event of the people who invited him. Even if he didn't have time, he used to find time.

There's a very deep lesson here. I realized how important it is for people to be there for others. One may be rich or poor, but an invitation should be accepted graciously. If you've given your word, keep it. No matter what. A simple gesture like turning up when you have promised, reaching when you said you would, or doing something you promised to do, says a lot about your personality. It's a gesture that gives people the willingness to trust you. There's respect, honour and faith in your word.

Even if you're merely turning up to brighten someone's day, it means a lot. I have witnessed Sahab reaching out to people in response to their invitation. It could be a friend's daughter's wedding, and he would show up, ready to stand on stage and greet the newlywed couple, give them his blessings. It was always great to watch them shower him with love in return.

As individuals, how many times do we go to the weddings of people who serve us or help us in our household work? Or their offspring's events? How many times do we inquire about the lives of the people who serve and help us? Have we stopped and asked that employee how's everything at home? We run: run from conversation and run from confrontation.

When I started my first business, it was my baby. I hired a few people and they worked for me, but it was still my company. I never realized that I wasn't truly appreciating them for the hard work they put in, day in and day out. My employees treated my company as their own baby.

One day Sahab had asked me about one of my employees. To my horror, and his, I didn't know the answer. That day, Sahab said to me, "Our world is made of people. Don't neglect them. Respect them. Only then will they respect you back. Live for them, and they'll live for you."

It is one of the best things I've learnt from Sahab. When I applied this to my company, it soared. I focused on warmth when talking to my staff, I appreciated their hard work and genuinely tried to connect with them. As a leader, I have learnt to study people, their likes, their strengths, and eventually help boost them to reach their true potential.

Every time a new employee joins the team, it is like a new addition to the family, and every time someone leaves, we bid goodbye like we were sending off a family member, wishing them the best for their new adventure.

When you understand the people around you, when you talk to them and listen to them, you form deeper connections. They don't quit your company because they are unhappy. They may have a personal issue in their life or they may be feeling lonely, or sometimes they leave when it is time for them to further spread their wings. They leave when they themselves are ready to find the next big move for them.

That's the culture I adopt. And that's another lesson that I had from Dilip Sahab.

"You are not just your profession. You are a human being. You should always give back to people. Spend a part of your time helping people who don't have privileges like you do," Dilip Sahab always used to say.

In all the years I'd known Sahab, he always encouraged me to help people. "We are all answerable to the almighty. When our time on earth is over, the Lord will ask us what we have done for this world and how many smiles did we spread. That day, our heads should not hang in shame. Live for others. You'll receive a lot of blessings."

11

Paani Puri and Other
Lessons with Sahab

Dilip Kumar was very particular about little things. If you were in his company, rest assured, he would make you feel well taken care of. Sahab would not let you out of his sight and would ensure people treat you the same way he was treated.

A few years ago, I had accompanied Dilip Sahab to an event. I had attended a few such high-profile events as the one we were going to, but never with a superstar. I was silently hoping there wouldn't be a mob similar to the one I had encountered at the airport a few years earlier.

When we reached, I heaved a sigh of relief seeing the crowd at a significant distance and the security alert and efficient. The valet opened the car door for us and I followed Sahab out of his sleek Mercedes.

There was heavy security at the gate, and the crowd looked dignified. They made way for the superstar politely. His fans looked at him adoringly, but no one made a vexatious attempt to interact with Dilip Sahab. There was a huge crowd but it was managed well.

Dilip Sahab, being the dignitary, sailed right through the security checkpoints. Unfortunately for me, I got stuck behind the crowd. We got separated. Resigned, I took my place in the queue with the other attendees and watched from a distance as Sahab's silhouette disappeared around the corner.

I waited patiently as the people in front of me were frisked. The queue made slow progress and I was slightly disappointed at being left behind. Hardly two people had cleared through when a man in a crisp black suit walked up and announced my name in a loud clear voice.

"Mr Faisal Farooqui."

I moved towards him and introduced myself. He asked me to follow him, and we walked down the same hall Dilip Sahab had disappeared. This time, I was given the same quick security clearance as Sahab had been. The man in front of me walked swiftly, and I kept up with him. Within minutes, we had caught up with Dilip Sahab. He turned around and welcomed me back with a warm smile.

He then faced the security head and instructed him firmly about how it was going to go from here on. "He is my guest. He's come with me. Wherever I go, he will come along with me. You cannot leave him behind like that."

The security head apologized profusely to him and to me.

"You don't have to apologize to us. Please make sure it is not repeated. My guests are important to me. They are to be treated the same way as I am."

It was one of the reasons I grew close to Sahab. He respected me. He would make sure that whenever I was with him, I would be treated like priority. And not just me, whoever was with him, would be given priority.

I have witnessed so many people accompanying other high-profile guests, but receiving second-grade treatment, while the star enjoys the pleasures of being pampered. With Dilip Sahab, everybody felt like a star unto themselves. I, personally, have never seen him distinguish between people based on their economic or social standing. Whatever your profession, your work speaks for you.

He would often tell me, "You see, everybody works. I also work. The only difference between my work and their work is that my work gets showcased on TV and on screen. Everyone works hard. No one is big or small here."

Dilip Sahab always walked his talk. There is not one thing he said to me that he himself didn't truly believe in and follow. And this was true of whatever situation or condition he found himself in. I remember another incident that revealed his magnanimous nature even in the midst of a personal tragedy.

Dilip Sahab's mother-in-law, Naseem Banu, passed away in June 2002. Naseem Banu was one of India's first big names in the movie industry. She started her acting career sometime around 1930 and with a small hiatus in the 1940s, she remained at the top until her last movie in 1957. Legend has it that she was so strikingly beautiful that Naushad Sahab nicknamed her *pari-chehra* (fairy face). Separated from her husband in 1947, she provided her two children with the best of education and values. She raised them to be strong, independent, hard-working, and humble adults.

Being just a few years older than Dilip Sahab, the two shared a dignified friendship that was only strengthened by Sahab and Saira baji's marriage. Her demise saddened Sahab immensely.

I received the call about Naseem Banu's death from Dilip Sahab at about 7:30 a.m. It was 18 June, and the morning had turned sad. Dilip Sahab's voice seemed distant.

"Faisal, the funeral procession will depart before the *zohar* prayer time. You should come early though and stay by my side."

I shared the sad news at home, texted a few people who I felt should know about the passing away of Naseem Banu, and then got ready. I reached Dilip Sahab's home at 9 a.m. and as was expected, there were hundreds of people already present to offer their condolences to the family. I made my way through the crowd. I went up to Sahab and embraced him, offering him my condolences.

The tradition in Islam dictates that men and women must mourn separately and this held me back from meeting Saira baji. My heart hurt for her loss. Sahab indicated that I sit on the couch beside him, and so I sat there quietly, patiently, holding his hand, as he accepted condolences from the mourners.

Naseem Banu's burial was carried out at the Juhu-Santa Cruz mosque. On our way back, Dilip Sahab, despite knowing that I had my car with me, insisted that I travel with him.

"Sahab, please don't worry. Please go ahead. I have my car. We will meet at home."

Dilip Sahab got into his car and it started pulling out of the crowded street outside the mosque. They had just driven a few metres before abruptly coming to a halt. The window rolled down, and Sahab turned to look for me. I was standing on the road, waiting for my driver to bring my car.

While I was on the phone, coordinating with my driver, Sahab spotted me and once again asked me to come with him.

"You sure your car is here?"

Here sat a legend, vulnerable after the loss of a loved one, but still remembering to ask me about my comfort and making sure that I reached home without any trouble.

Sahab and I often used to drive down to a local shop for a plate of mouth-watering, sweet and spicy paani puri. He would pick me up in his maroon Mercedes and we would head to Karachi Sweets, which was then situated opposite St Stanislaus School at Hill Road in Bandra. We used to pull up next to the shop. The owner, receptive and accommodating of Sahab, would notice the car and send his best employee with plates of paani puri. Sahab would never exit his car. He was aware that the sheer number of people who would crowd outside Karachi Sweets just to meet him would overwhelm the store and the employees trying to run it.

On one lovely summer evening of 2004, Sahab said, "Let's have paani puri by the sea today."

So, we decided to stop by for a plate of paani puri at the sea-facing coffee shop at Taj Land's End. Formerly known as the Regent's Hotel, it was built and owned by Siraj Lokhandwala. One of the most beautiful locations in Mumbai, Regent's Hotel suffered major financial losses, and eventually, the Lokhandwala family sold the property to India's Taj Group of Hotels in late 2002.

Before we could find a table and settle down, people started approaching us, trying to meet Dilip Sahab. A thorough gentleman, after the first ten minutes of meet and greet, Sahab pointed towards me and said, "Meet him. He's my friend. He's very hungry, so I've brought him here so that we eat something. Please allow us to eat."

Everyone smiled at us respectfully and we were given some privacy to enjoy our meal. We ordered two plates of paani puri. It was delicious. After we were done, Sahab requested for the bill. The manager came to our table and said, "Sir, it is our honour that you have graced us with your presence. We could never ask you to pay."

Sahab was a man of honour himself, and I knew that he wouldn't leave without paying the bill, so I decided to have a word with the manager privately.

"I understand you don't want to offer Dilip Kumar the bill, but he won't leave without paying. He will never accept not paying for the food he's eating at a restaurant. He'll just get unnecessarily upset."

The manager finally gave in and assured me that he would personally bring the bill to our table in a few minutes. I headed back with a smile. When the cheque arrived, I habitually reached out for the small leather folder to pay. A slightly stunned Dilip Kumar stopped me.

"Why will you pay? I am older than you. I will pay the bill."

He opened the soft folder, picked up the smooth long piece of paper, and for a minute, just stared at the amount. When he put the bill down to take out his wallet, I picked up the bill. Each plate of paani puri costed us 250 rupees. Sahab pulled a face and said, "Five hundred rupees for paani puri. Karachi Sweets on Hill Road serves better paani puri for just twenty rupees a plate."

I chuckled at his reaction. A man of his stature could afford to buy each ingredient for a thousand rupees every single day of his life without flinching, but it was expensive for a plate of paani puri. The hard-working man inside him who grew up in Peshawar and Deolali and learned the value of hard-earned money in the canteens of Pune and the studios of Bombay, couldn't reconcile himself to the exorbitant amount being charged for something that was available at a fraction of the price elsewhere.

"All the money we earn involves hard work. If you don't put the work into it, you don't respect it. Work hard, earn your living. You'll always be proud of it, and you'll never spend it on trivial things." Yet another lesson from this most unassuming of men.

12

Nehru's Hero: In the Service of the Nation

After Independence, while India came to be politically governed by the Congress, Indian cinema was being ruled by the big three – Raj Kapoor, Dev Anand and Dilip Kumar. They were called 'the golden trio' of Indian cinema. Having started their careers in the 1940s, they were the biggest stars of the era. Each of the superstars had their own fan following and worshippers. Men would want to be them, and women would want to be with them.

I remember one evening, while enjoying tea with Dilip Sahab and Saira baji in their lawn, I asked them who among the three was the most popular among the ladies. Dilip Sahab chuckled and looked at Saira baji, who grinned back with a naughty twinkle in her eye.

"Raj and I weren't very popular with the ladies. Dev was. He would always talk about some or the other lady who was fawning over him."

Saira baji, quick as ever, immediately quipped, "But who knows? He (Dev Anand) did have a propensity to exaggerate his claims and humour us all the time."

Dilip Sahab and Saira baji turned to look at each other and broke into an adorable laugh. I suddenly felt like an outsider who wasn't privy to an inside joke that the two age-old close friends in front of me shared. I looked at them and I couldn't help but smile and then I laughed along.

The media used to claim that there was fierce competition among the golden trio but in reality, Dilip Kumar, Raj Kapoor and Dev Anand were close friends. Together, they had widespread influence over the masses. Prime Minister Jawaharlal Nehru understood this and used their influence in an intelligent way.

After Independence, people were still reeling from the after effects of the Partition. Millions were mourning the losses of their loved ones. There was distrust and destruction everywhere. Refugee camps were overflowing with people. My mother and uncles would often narrate the horror stories they read in the newspapers or incidents they had heard from survivors who lived to tell their tales. Those were very strange times. People had turned into animals. "So many times, it felt like the world was ending," my mother would often say.

I would look at them and see the horror and fear in their eyes while they recounted the stories. I am sure millions have read articles and heard stories about the devastating and long trauma of Partition on both sides. We have all, at some point in life, discussed the horrors our ancestors faced. They truly were strange times.

I never asked Dilip Sahab why his family never went back to Peshawar. Years later Sahab's visit to Pakistan in 1989 became the talk of the town. He visited his Peshawar home and witnessed his dilapidated house. Once I asked him if he ever considered going back and remaking the home he grew up in.

"*Ma'ashra dil se banta hai, makanaat se nahi.*" (Environment is created by hearts, not by houses.) His belief, that a home is where the heart is, struck a chord with me. His millions of admirers, well-wishers and fans all over the world perhaps made Dilip Kumar feel at home wherever he stayed.

Jawaharlal Nehru and many others were rallying to create safe travel routes for people who were leaving their homes and crossing the borders. Families required shelter, encouragement to begin their lives again in a newly independent but divided nation, a support system to help deal with the losses they faced, and a boost to their flagging morale. The government needed young icons to help spread the message of peace and positivity among the public. It decided that there were no better icons than the golden trio.

Dilip Sahab made a number of trips to Delhi for work-related assignments and of course to help lift the spirit of a nation. He often met the prime minister, and worked tirelessly to restore some semblance of normalcy to a society reeling from the aftermath of the madness that Partition had engendered.

I had never asked Sahab much, but gathering from what he had told me, Jawaharlal Nehru was like a father figure him. Pandit Nehru or Pandit-ji, as he was popularly called, was a voracious reader and was well-informed about the society and its cultures and was definitely a man connected to his roots. He probably saw a bit of himself in the young Yusuf Khan. Among the golden trio, Jawaharlal Nehru personally loved Dilip Sahab's company a lot. There were standing instructions from Pandit Nehru that whenever Dilip Sahab visited Delhi, he was to have breakfast with the prime minister and his family at their residence. Dilip Sahab truly was Nehru's hero.

One fine evening, Dilip Sahab lovingly enacted to me how Pandit Nehru would ask his daughter, Indira Gandhi, to serve him eggs and toast. He sat up straight, wrinkled his face, and spoke in an authoritarian voice and style. "Indira, serve some toast to Yusuf. His plate is empty. How can he leave without eating."

I couldn't help but smile at his childlike enthusiasm, and the precision with which he nailed Jawaharlal Nehru's mannerisms.

In 1998, Dilip Sahab was awarded the Nishan-e-Imtiaz by the Government of Pakistan for excellence in his field. Being the highest civilian award in Pakistan, the Nishan-e-Imtiaz is awarded to a person who has achieved success and eminence in an area. As the news spread, there was commotion among the Indian diaspora. Dilip Sahab's acceptance of an award from Pakistan was considered disrespectful by some people in India. A group of people would shout slogans outside his home, demanding he return the award. Dilip Sahab refused to buckle under such personal heckling. He wrote to the then prime minister of India, Atal Bihari Vajpayee, and penned down his thoughts on the matter. He also assured the prime minister of his love for the country, and stated that if his accepting the award was against the country's interest, he would return the award in a heartbeat. Mr Vajpayee promptly met Dilip Sahab.

Atal Bihari Vajpayee, being a wise leader, recognized Dilip Sahab's years of contribution to cinema and the nation. He was quoted saying, "There is no doubt about film star Dilip Kumar's patriotism and commitment to the nation."

Prime Minister Atal Bihari Vajpayee had always been a fan of Dilip Sahab's work. As Sahab was bestowed with this honour by the Government of Pakistan, the prime ministers of the two countries moved further towards bringing the two nations together. Dilip Sahab's relationship and personal respect for the prime minister prompted Mr Vajpayee to approach him, offering him the position of an emissary charged with handling backdoor diplomacy with the Pakistan government.

Dilip Sahab's charm and personality were well known across the globe. His fans were present in every industry, including not only the prime minister of India, but also the prime minister of Pakistan, Nawaz Sharif. Upon India's request, Dilip Sahab travelled to London where he met the prime minister of Pakistan.

Personally, I wasn't privy to any information or conversation that took place in London, but I was happily informed that Nawaz Sharif had a fanboy moment while meeting Dilip Sahab. He had lovingly asked him to repeat his movie dialogues and Sahab had obliged. Nawaz Sharif was loosely quoted saying, "If Dilip Kumar is the ambassador of peace from India's side, I will ensure that Pakistan will make every effort to reach a peace treaty."

Sahab's humble contribution perhaps played a role that resulted in signing of the Lahore Declaration, a bilateral agreement and governance treaty signed between Pakistan and India on 21 February 1999.

Dilip Sahab was never really interested in politics. He supported the government, and rallied for various causes, but never fully participated in the political scenario. This was until he was approached by Sonia Gandhi, leader of the Congress party and soon to be elected leader of the Opposition in India's Parliament.

After her husband, the former prime minister Rajiv Gandhi's assassination in 1991, his wife, and the rock of the Gandhi family, Sonia Gandhi, refused to get involved in politics. Subsequently, the party's leadership yielded to P.V. Narasimha Rao as the prime minister of the country (1991-96). After the electoral loss of 1996, the Congress party had begun to disintegrate. Many veterans, lured by their own agenda, quit and the party was in danger of being sidelined by other political parties. With much reluctance, and in an attempt to breathe new life into the country's politics and the Congress party, Sonia Gandhi joined the party in 1997, and was soon elected as its president in 1998. It was now time for her to contest the Lok Sabha elections of 1999.

Due to her foreign origin, many people, some even within her own party, were against her position as the party president. She faced resistance, and required assistance to rally for her. This is when she reached out to Dilip Kumar, who had once helped her late husband's grandfather, Pandit Nehru.

I sat beside Sahab and intently listened as he narrated the time he met Sonia Gandhi in Delhi.

"She called me around the time when she was elected as the Congress president. There's one thing she said which made my heart bleed."

She had asked him, "Dilip Sahab, even you have left us?" Dilip Kumar had discerned the feeling of being 'letdown' in her voice.

Sahab promised her that he will never forsake them. He assured her that he had stood by the Congress party since the pre-independence days when he was arrested in Pune for participating in the Quit India Movement in 1942.

"She asked me to help rally the masses for the party for the approaching general elections. I was aware that she was actively participating in reinvigorating the Congress party. Anyway, when she asked, I had to step up for the party and for the nation."

In the general elections of 1999, Dilip Kumar was Congress party's star campaigner. Along with Asif bhai, he extensively crisscrossed constituencies in urban and rural India. Although the final results brought in a BJP-led government, Sonia Gandhi became the leader of the Opposition, a graceful, humble politician, and a leader of the masses.

Dilip Sahab displayed excellence during his campaign of 1999. Before we knew it, in 2000, the Congress party convinced him to formally accept a nomination to the Rajya Sabha, a position he held for one term until 2006.

One day in 2002, we reached Jogger's Park a little earlier than usual. People were still around. Sahab stopped every few feet to meet and greet some fan or admirer. I wondered why we had come so early. It was unusual and inconvenient, as Sahab would frequently point out to me. Eventually, the crowd thinned out. By the time we had taken one whole circle, it was closing time. The security walked around the park, asking the remaining people to leave. They knew Sahab would be staying back another hour.

We had finished our walk and stopped to rest at one of the benches. Sahab seemed a bit distracted. He was lost in thoughts and I didn't know whether to ask him what was on his mind.

"I have worked my entire life. I've served my family, the industry and the nation. I've earned a lot for myself through the years through hard work and passion."

It was quiet except for the sound of the waves crashing against the rocks. The moon was full. I could see the moonlight bounce off the water in the distance, shimmering like a thousand diamonds thrown on a bed of black velvet. Under the glow of the park lights, combined with the shine of the moonlight, Sahab's face looked wise, like he knew something of extreme significance.

I knew better than to ask him what was on his mind. If he wanted to, Sahab would have shared it with me. As I looked at him, he turned and looked at me with a smile that seemed to know some mighty secret.

"Some very honourable and senior people from Delhi have been reaching out to me for the past few weeks regarding some political work. I love the opportunities to contribute my ideas to help as many people as possible."

"There's always something we can all do. It's a lifetime of giving," I had said.

"You're right, which is why I want to give more. As much as I can."

"Sahab, you have always worked hard for the masses. And you continue to do so much more. You receive crores of blessings."

After a brief silence, I brought him back to the subject, "You were saying something about Delhi, Sahab."

"Yes, so some people have approached me and said that they want to…"

Sahab paused mid-sentence. I could sense he was trying to hint at something, but his pause was longer than usual. I couldn't bear the suspense.

"What was it?"

"I am going to tell you what it was but as of now please keep this strictly confidential. Please don't mention it to anyone."

"Yes, Sahab, absolutely."

I could see he was a bit indecisive, a rare sight that I had never seen before.

"They want me to give them my consent for the presidential elections."

"President of?" I asked in astonishment.

"India," replied Sahab.

It took my mind a few minutes to process what Dilip Sahab had said.

Sahab looked at my confused face and the amusement on his face was an apt reply.

"Sahab, I honestly don't know what to say. This is such a huge opportunity."

"I am aware of that. And if it makes you feel better, I had the same expression on my face as yours when I realized what they were hinting at. It struck me after they had left, and I have been quiet since then."

"Did they ask you directly?"

"No, they hinted at it."

It was a big moment in all our lives, especially Sahab and Saira baji. They would have to move to Delhi, change their lifestyle, and make other compromises that came along with the responsibility.

"So, if they ask you, will you agree?"

"I don't know. I haven't decided yet."

"Why not? Are there any hurdles? Because this is a huge honour."

"I know. I will have to speak with Saira and the others. More importantly, I don't know how equipped I am to handle something of this nature. I've never requested or asked favours or anything for myself from anybody."

"What would you have to ask for?"

Before I could finish the statement, Sahab's amused look had faded away and the earlier distracted look returned. He didn't respond and I knew the conversation had ended. We eventually left and after a pleasant and warm goodbye, I headed home.

Back then, when I went over our conversation after reaching home, I realized that it would be in the interests of all political parties if Sahab were to accept the position. He would be accessible to both political alliances in the Parliament (the UPA and the NDA) and his primary concern would be the well-being of the people. As a man of the world, a star, an icon of the masses, a man of several accomplishments, there was no doubt in my mind that he would be the ideal choice as our country's president.

As the days passed, Sahab started talking less about the Rajya Sabha and politics in general. The summer was almost gone and the first heavy rains were threatening to wash the city. Evenings had become more pleasant. I could look up and see the clouds slowly rolling in. They looked proud and menacing.

Soon after, we were at Jogger's Park again. It was a few minutes to nine, and we were ready to begin our walk under the soft glow of the lamps. I love those lamps. They provide such an undefinable sense of comfort. I've had many conversations with a number of people under those lights, most significant being the ones with Dilip Sahab. Their glow has made so many conversations seem surreal in my mind, the presidential conversation being one of them. Tonight, under a cloudy sky, I was going to ask him about the presidency again.

"Sahab, did you ever end up saying yes to those representatives from Delhi?"

"Yes for what?"

Sahab looked at me with mild confusion on his face. I realized I was being slightly vague.

"For the presidency," I explained.

Sahab turned away from me. There was that distant look in his eyes. He was looking at the pathway in front of him as he walked forward with his hands held together behind his back. The top button on the mandarin collar of his white kurta was open, and in that moment, I remember thinking, if anyone deserved the position of the president of India, it was him.

There was an aura about him. I could picture him taking his evening walks in the gardens of Rashtrapati Bhavan. Sahab would love the flowers that bloom every spring there. He would enjoy the chill of the Delhi winter and the warmth of the summers. He would enjoy the quiet of the vast grounds. And most importantly, he would enjoy serving the people of the country and the Constitution of the land he always had so much love for.

"No, I didn't. I thought about it. They were hinting that if I want it, I would have to talk to all the political leaders, lobby for it. It would have been a great opportunity, but I'm sure there's someone out there who's more suited for this responsibility."

"If you don't mind me asking, why not lobby?"

"*Chhodo yaar. Inke unke paas jaa kar khud ki sifarish karana mujhe nahin aata.*" (Let it go. I don't know how to go to people and advocate for myself.)

I could sense the irritation. Sahab had used the word 'yaar' with me the first time. I decided it would be best if I cut short the discussion.

I assumed they had requested that he approach certain senior leader(s) in the government and the Opposition, and ask for their support.

I realized that Sahab was not someone to go out seeking favours. His Pathan values were too deeply ingrained, and he would in no manner bow down in front of anyone. Through the years, I had watched as he campaigned and rallied for the people's benefits. He had raised money for charities and spread awareness of arts, literature and education and devoted his energies towards social causes. But Sahab was stubborn. His principles stopped him from asking for favours for himself, or allow himself to be in situations where you succeed at the mercy of others. He would have gone to any length to serve others, but he would never compromise on his values.

A few weeks later, on 25 July 2002, A.P.J. Abdul Kalam became the president of India. He held the post from 2002 to 2007, with support from the ruling and the Opposition alliances. Sahab was overjoyed to see that a man of such substance had been elected as the country's president. When the announcement was made, I had to rush to Sahab's house to speak with him. He seemed satisfied.

"The position of the president of a country is a massive responsibility. It takes a certain talent, precision, understanding and maturity to successfully lead at this position without breaking down. I think Dr Kalam will do an exceptional job."

Sahab's brush with real politics was brief, but he always kept himself aware of what was going on. Right from the beginning, he had involved himself in activities in service of the of the people, without compromising his values or self-esteem..

13

Saira Banu and Family

At the age of forty-four, Dilip Kumar married Saira Banu, a twenty-two-year-old beauty who was a superstar in her own right. The country went crazy with joy. It was the talk of the town. Everyone had an opinion about it. From the very get-go it was obvious that Dilip Kumar and Saira Banu were destined to be together. It was a match made in heaven. A fairy-tale romance.

One evening, just as I was getting ready to meet Sahab at his home, I received a call from him.

"Have you left home yet?"

"No, Sahab. I was just about to step out. Where are you?"

"I'm at home. You wait there. We are coming to pick you up."

"Ok, Sahab. I'll wait for you."

It was strange. Usually, I used to go to Sahab's home first. It took Sahab less than ten minutes to reach my place. I rushed downstairs and sat beside him on the back seat. In the driver's seat was Kutti, Sahab's trusted driver for decades, and beside him sat a constable from Mumbai Police.

Since 1998, whenever Sahab stepped out of his house, he was accompanied by a pilot car full of armed officers and constables of the Mumbai Police.

After I entered the car, Sahab requested the security personnel to shift to the pilot car as he wanted to discuss something private with me. His tone was slightly curt. He seemed to be in a bad mood. So, while the well-built policeman in the black safari suit meekly protested, he eventually agreed to leave us alone.

"As-salamu alaikum, how are you, Sahab?"

"I am ok. But I am also not ok."

"What happened, Sahab?"

"Nothing."

Instead of heading to Jogger's Park, Sahab instructed Kutti to turn the car around and head back home. We reached his house and sat in the foyer of his bungalow at 34/B Pali Hill.

Not expecting to see us back so soon, Saira baji walked up to us and, with genuine surprise on her face, inquired about our evening.

"How come you are back so soon? Didn't you guys go for your walk?"

It had seemed like a harmless question to me, but it irked Sahab. Soon, a brief argument in hushed tones ensued. Saira baji was insisting that he go for a walk, and Sahab was adamant about not doing so. Eventually, he turned to me.

"You tell me. Would my mother ever speak to my father in this manner?"

Not wanting to take sides, I simply kept mum. Sahab heaved a huge sigh and gave up on the argument.

"Come, let's go for our walk."

Shoulders slumped and having just lost an argument, Sahab slowly walked back to the car. I stayed two steps behind. As the car proceeded from Pali Hill towards the narrow lanes that led to Carter Road, Sahab looked at me.

"Saira is after my life."

"What happened, Sahab?"

"She keeps telling me to go for a walk, as if I am a kid."

I tried to hide a smile. It was adorable. I looked at Sahab and pictured the conversation between him and Saira baji. She had probably pointed out that he was getting lazy and he had stormed out with a grumpy face, loudly announcing that he was going for a walk. I wanted to laugh out loud at the silliness and the love and care they shared.

"Sahab, she cares for you, that's why she says it."

"I know that. But every day? I am eighty years old. She keeps telling me every day as if I'm a child."

I studied the scowl on his face. He reminded me of a child being forced to do his homework. His creases appeared deeper and his frown looked like it was going to stay there forever. His soft wrinkled skin had a tinge of red from anger.

We reached Jogger's Park and had hardly walked a few metres when he abruptly said, "Let's head back to the car."

Considering his mood, I quietly obliged. I called Kutti and we walked back to his car. I wasn't sure where we were heading. We just seemed to be driving around Bandra aimlessly. After about an hour, Sahab turned to Kutti.

"Tell me, how many rounds of the park did we take today, four or five?"

Kutti broke into laughter. "Five," he guessed. Amused at the situation, I turned to Sahab and said we had walked six rounds, not five. All of us were chuckling by then.

"Oh, you counted? We took six rounds? Ok, so we walked six rounds today. If Saira asks, don't forget to tell her that."

As Kutti agreed and obliged, I couldn't help but fall more in love with Sahab. He was still a bit grumpy, but there was a hint of a smile on his face. A satisfied smile. He was obstinate about not walking and he had got his way. We ended up driving around Bandra for a while, and then he dropped me home.

This incident has been etched into my memory ever since. People crave the romance of candlelight, flowers and gifts but I think this is what real romance is. A woman insisting and fighting for her husband's health and the small arguments that stem from years of adulation and love.

It takes a different kind of strength to walk through life with the same person beside you, day after day, night after night.

Dilip Sahab and Saira baji's marriage was probably the biggest Bollywood news of its time. Many people had predicted that the marriage of a forty-four-year-old man with a twenty-two-year-old girl would not go well. Women across the country had mourned, as Dilip Kumar, the man of their dreams, was no longer single. Saira baji once told me how the postman would deliver letters written in blood, of women professing their undying love for Dilip Kumar and expressing their anger towards her for marrying him.

"It's hard to believe the kind of love people showered on him. It left me in awe and sometimes even scared me. I love my husband, and it's only after we got married that I saw the real magnitude of his popularity."

Their relationship passed the one test most don't. It passed the test of time. The people who did not approve of the relationship when they got married eventually started to love their relationship. At the time, they were what we call today #couplegoals.

Saira Banu was born on 23 August 1944, in a family of nawabs and artists. Her mother was an actress and her grandmother was a renowned singer and musician. Being born in a family with such a deep connect with the world of art, Saira baji, even as a child, wanted to enter the world of movies. Her love for Dilip Kumar, which she harboured in her heart from the time she was merely twelve, only strengthened her resolve to join the film industry.

Naseem Banu, Saira baji's mother, had married Mian Ehsan-ul-Haq, and together had started a film production house named Taj Mahal Pictures. They had two children. Their first child was Sultan, born in 1939, followed by Saira five years later.

After Partition, Mian Ehsan-ul-Haq decided to migrate to Pakistan, while Naseem Banu chose to stay back in India. Mian Ehsan-ul-Haq packed up and left, eventually settling in Vienna, Austria. When he left, he took the film rolls he jointly owned with his wife, and released them in Pakistan. So, after her husband left, Naseem Banu was completely broke, with hardly any resource to take care of her children. She had quit acting to raise Sultan and Saira, but her husband's abandonment forced her to start working again in 1948. She last acted in *Nausherwan-E-Adil* (1957) starring Sohrab Modi.

To make sure her children received a good education, Naseem Banu and her mother temporarily moved to London. Soon, she returned to India while leaving her children with their grandmother. Mian Ehsan-ul-Haq wanted to meet their children but Naseem Banu refused to entertain his wishes. She continued to live her life, working hard and earning for her family. Naseem Banu grieved her husband's abandonment till the very end.

A few years after their separation, Mian Ehsan-ul-Haq married an Austrian woman while in Vienna, and spent most of his time shuttling between Austria and Pakistan, rarely coming to India to meet his family.

I met Saira baji's father only once, at Jogger's Park. Sahab had reached the park by 5.30 p.m. and had asked me to come by. I had wrapped up work as fast as I could, and reached Jogger's Park half an hour later.

I had found them near one of Sahab's favourite benches by the sea. Sahab seemed to have completed his walk. Usually, Sahab was in the company of two armed policemen, but that day, there was also an old man with a black cane present. He leaned heavily on the cane..

When Sahab noticed me, he smiled and signalled to me to join them on the bench. As I got closer, I noticed that the man beside Sahab had a royal demeanour. His face was lined with deep creases. He looked quite stern, like someone I would think twice before saying anything to. His black cane had a regal design on it, as if making a statement of its own.

Sahab introduced him to me.

"He is Saira's father, Mr Ehsan-ul-Haq. He'll be staying with us for a few days."

I was slightly taken aback. In all the years I had known Sahab and Saira baji, I had never heard them speak about him.

A few days after Mian Ehsan-ul-Haq left, I was at Dilip Sahab's home and he was teasing Saira baji.

"So, tell me, do you know who Saira's father is? He's a very short-tempered man. Oh well, you've met him at the park."

Sahab had a twinkle in his eyes as he waited for his wife's reaction. "You're no less," Saira baji shot back, smiling at Sahab, before turning around with a regal and graceful demeanour that matched her father's and walking away. Sahab and I burst into a soft laughter.

Saira baji has a lot of similarities with her mother. She has the strength of an independent woman, and the dedication of a homemaker. She, like her mother, quit her acting career shortly after marriage to take care of her husband and their family. She has lived for Dilip Sahab.

There were similarities between her father and Dilip Sahab too. Although of a very jolly nature, Sahab used to be quite stern at times and lose his temper. Perhaps that's why Saira Banu fell madly in love with Dilip Kumar despite him being twenty-two years older.

Saira Banu, perhaps, found in Dilip Kumar what she couldn't find in her father. There was comfort, safety and security of knowing that your husband is yours and will be there for you till the end of time.

I asked Sahab and Saira baji if they had asked Mian Ehsan-ul-Haq sahab to stay back for a few more days. Dilip Sahab had looked at his wife and smiled. His heart hurt for her. Despite the resentment she had for abandoning them, she was after all a daughter. And a daughter always misses her father. It's a bond that cannot be replaced by any other man in the world. For a woman, her father is her king.

"Mian Ehsan sahab hardly comes here. He had come for a few days to spend time with us. I requested him to extend his stay for a few more days, but he didn't."

Years later, when Mian Ehsan passed away, Saira baji reflected on the short time she got to spend with her father. Each time, Dilip Sahab had taken care of him, made sure he was comfortable and treated him with respect. Her love and respect for Sahab had only grown owing to this.

Despite not having a father figure around, Saira baji had a very comfortable life. Naseem Banu didn't leave any stone unturned in taking care of her children. In fact, she raised her children in luxury. They received exceptional education in London. When they returned to Bombay in 1960, Saira was taken by the world of glamour and cinema. Although Naseem Banu was against it in the beginning, she eventually gave in, and Saira Banu made her debut as an actress at the age of sixteen. A few years later, in 1966, she married the superstar whom she, in her own words, 'loved since she was a little girl'.

They were always protective and loving of each other, but in the last few years, their love had grown stronger. Every time I used to see them together, I wondered how much love must a person have to care about the other so much. Despite having an army of helpers in the house, Saira baji was always hands-on when it came to taking care of Sahab. She has always said, "Dilip sahab is my king, my emperor, my Kohinoor."

"Saira baji, how do you do all this? It is so powerful. Where did you learn how to take care of someone like this?" I had once asked her.

"Faisal, this is not really something you can learn. It comes from within and if your heart isn't in it, you're not going to do it properly in any case."

I waited and watched her as she sorted out Sahab's shirts. She was helping arrange his clothes according to shades. I watched, waiting for her to continue. I knew she had more to say.

"My mother would tell me often, 'Saira, take care of this man. He's a gem. Don't lose him.' I was taught how to give my best. Wherever or whatever it may be. And he's my husband. I love him. I don't know how one can't do all this. It's so basic. When you love someone, it just comes naturally. You don't have to think. It's not a chore. I love taking care of Sahab."

She gave an all-knowing smile and looked at Sahab adoringly. That face was not just beautiful, it was also wise. She had lived her life for her family, especially her husband, and it showed.

She used to walk into the kitchen to ensure that Sahab's food was made exactly how he liked it. Till the very end, she used to make sure that he had a white handkerchief with a hand-embroidered 'DK' on it.

Through thick and thin, she was right there with him, supporting him, encouraging him, helping him.

Once, when Sahab, Saira baji and I were walking in the park, he slowed down and let Saira baji walk a few steps ahead of us. Looking towards me, he said, "Allah is kind to me by blessing me with such a wonderful woman in my life. Sometimes I wonder what my life would have been without her, and there's only one answer – it wouldn't even be a life without her by my side."

Sahab, having grown up in a large family, had always loved families staying together. He used to love when large families sat together in the evenings, bonding over meals and tea. Whenever kids used to accompany us to their home, I could see Dilip Sahab and Saira baji overjoyed to mingle with them.

Dilip Sahab used to make faces at the kids and they made faces right back. It's a little game they used to play.

Unfortunately, the beautiful couple was never blessed with a child. I never asked them why. It seemed too personal to ask, but I do know one thing – they did want children. It is probably because of this reason that Sahab was like a father-figure to so many.

During the early 1980s, tabloids and film magazines were running stories about Dilip Kumar marrying a woman by the name of Asma Sahiba, a socialite hailing from Hyderabad. I'd heard several accounts from people, most surrounding Saira baji's inability to conceive, but I never believed it was a topic worth broaching. As it turned out, I didn't have to ask.

Once Sahab was a bit under the weather when I went to visit him. I held his hand – I used to love holding his hand and sit with him. Saira baji was nearby. When tea was served, she asked me to get comfortable at the table. I obliged. We were generally talking when suddenly the topic of Asma came up.

Saira baji was busy helping Sahab dip biscuits in his tea and feeding it to him. She looked beautiful under the bright yellow of the light in the living room. She reminded me of my mother. I looked at her and smiled.

"Are Sahab and you all right?"

Saira baji smiled. She would rarely let her expressions give away what she was feeling, but that day seemed different. The air was crisp and quiet, almost eerie. A sense of loneliness hung in the air.

"Yes, we are. We have all these people around the house helping us. The most loyal staff, the best doctors."

"Yes, but are you ok? Doesn't it get lonely?"

"I'm sure it seems that way. We don't even have children. But then there's my brother's family and their children, and Sahab's nephews and nieces, you, and so many others, who keep coming home. It's almost like you are our children."

I smiled at her. I knew I felt the same. I saw wisdom in her eyes. On so many occasions, Sahab had held my hand and given me advice that helped me in my professional and personal life. He was more than a father to me.

"Dilip Sahab's sisters were keen on Sahab having children though. I myself was an accomplished actress, but we did not have our own children. I'm just glad I believed in my husband the way I did."

As I smiled, she narrated the incident to me. Dilip Sahab's sisters weren't the biggest fans of Saira Banu. As is the case with many families, the daughter-in-law had a hard time pleasing the in-laws. Sahab's sisters apparently created a hostile environment for Saira baji, making it difficult for her to go through even the most basic activities of the day. They annoyed and emotionally hurt Saira baji.

The family was obviously aware of Saira baji being unable to carry a child. One fateful day, they had found an opportunity to convince Dilip Sahab to get married again.

Crumbling under his siblings' persistence, Sahab agreed to marry Asma Sahiba. The marriage took place without Saira Banu having any knowledge of it. When she found out, as would be expected, she was upset and hurt. As a wife, she fought for her husband, but eventually gave in. She surrendered to the wishes of Dilip Kumar and his family. Dutifully, she continued to serve them and be the perfect wife and yet even more, a gracious bhabhi (sister-in-law) to sahab's siblings.

Dilip Sahab saw the hurt in his wife's eyes. She was sad and upset and although she was unwilling to share her husband with another woman, she had swallowed the bitter pill with strength and courage.

The fact that Dilip Kumar had married another woman didn't hurt her as much as the fact that he had hidden it from her. She believed that her husband trusted her and shared everything in his life with her. She hated that he had hidden something so important from her. She would tell him that if only he had talked to her about it, she wouldn't have been so hurt. She would have supported him in every way. His happiness was more important than anything else in the world for her.

I think it's one of the many reasons why Dilip Sahab loved her so much. She is the kind of woman who gives without asking. He hated seeing her sad and did whatever he could to see her smile.

One evening, while discussing it with Sahab, Saira baji burst into tears. She couldn't hold it in any more. That day, Sahab told her, "You are the most beautiful woman in the world. You are the most beautiful woman in my life. You have such a big heart and you're the kindest and the most caring person I have ever met. I cannot see you sad. It breaks my heart."

Dilip Sahab and Asma's marriage lasted less than two years. Over the years, Dilip Sahab and Saira baji forgot about the pain they felt during the two years of difficulty, but every now and then, Saira baji didn't let go of a chance to tease Sahab about it and his reaction every time was priceless.

His love for children was always evident. He used to tell me how happy he was that my brothers and I were blessed with such wonderful children, but he never regretted not having his own. He was more than happy in the relationship he shared with Saira baji.

14

Sahab's Family

To his siblings, Dilip Sahab was a father, a brother and a son. He had been the breadwinner and the man who, besides his parents and his older sister, had held his family together. Through thick and thin, he had been with them, and helped them live a peaceful and happy life.

As siblings do, they did have their own set of fights. But these outweighed the happy moments. The one thing they consistently did was be there for each other, and help each other through life.

Whenever I used to speak to Dilip Sahab about his siblings, I felt a sense of calm in his voice. It had been obvious that he had loved them a lot but at times, the way he spoke about them suggested that he, at times, also felt letdown by them. It could have also been a big brother's frustration with his siblings.

Ahsan bhai, after his education in the US, had come back to India. He had settled in Mumbai at 48 Pali Hill with Sahab. He hadn't married so as to dedicate his entire life to the family. Aslam bhai had chosen to stay back in the US, but forty-six years later, in 2001, having been through a divorce, he had returned to India to try and start a business.

Around 2005, Asif bhai and I were on our way to meet Dilip Sahab. We were told he was at his 48 Pali Hill bungalow. It was late afternoon, and a weekend. Since it's not often that Sahab would go there in the afternoons, we thought of surprising him instead of calling ahead.

As we walked up the stairs of the bungalow to reach the main floor, I could hear Sahab and his brothers, Ahsan and Aslam, in the middle of an argument. They were bickering like teenagers. I could clearly hear Ahsan bhai from the entrance.

"I have dedicated my whole life to you. What have you ever done for us?" I could hear Ahsan bhai say.

"Do you have no shame? What have I not done for you? I have given my life for you," was Dilip Sahab's reply.

Asif bhai and I looked at each other. We were sure that entering then would not be a good idea. I cleared my throat and shuffled my feet. They sensed our presence and stopped arguing.

We entered and greeted the three brothers. To say the environment was tense would be an understatement. I was shocked that they were speaking in loud tones with each other. The entire time that I had known them, both Aslam bhai and Ahsan bhai had always appeared happy and contented. I had never been formal with them in any sense, as both were like friends to me. With Dilip Sahab, I was always slightly formal because I worshipped him.

All of us gathered around the table in the middle of the painfully silent living room after the argument. Each of us sat quietly on the sofa. I kept my gaze fixed on the floor, as did the rest of them.

Eventually, Sahab broke the silence when he asked the house help to bring in some tea. The rest of the evening was marked by awkward silences and uncomfortable small talk.

A few days later, on a warm Sunday afternoon, I joined the three brothers for lunch. It was as if no fight had ever taken place among them. After lunch, Dilip Sahab retired to his room and I was alone with his brothers.

"So, you brothers also fight with each other..."

They laughed.

"What can we say? After all, we're brothers."

They proceeded to narrate to me an incident that made me laugh till I had tears in my eyes.

Sahab never shirked his responsibilities as the elder brother. As soon as he started earning, he began to provide for his family. They never had to ask him for anything. On her deathbed, Dilip Sahab had vowed to his mother that he would take care of all his siblings, especially his sisters. Dilip Sahab didn't leave any stone unturned when it came to taking care of his siblings. Ahsan bhai and Aslam bhai were enrolled in a local school in Bombay. Since Sahab was already a well-known public figure, they were treated like royalty there.

In 1955, after they completed their schooling, Ahsan bhai and Aslam bhai expressed their willingness to go abroad for further studies, away from the special treatment they were receiving in India. With great determination and hard work, both brothers got through an esteemed university in the US. Everyone in the family was proud of the two brothers.

During the 1950s, direct flights to Europe and America were not as convenient as they are today. Flights to the United States took almost seventy-two hours, including many stopovers along the way.

Ahsan bhai and Aslam bhai knew that the flight had a stopover at Beirut, Middle East's party capital, and wanted to experience the city.

Dilip Sahab, already well known across the globe, had a friend in Beirut. As a favour, Sahab's friend agreed to take care of his brothers during their stay in Beirut. A hotel room was booked for them and their food was taken care of.

Sahab's friend picked up the two boys from the airport and helped them safely check into their hotel. He left, telling them to contact him in case they needed anything. The two boys noted down his number, thanked him and bid him goodbye.

The teenagers had money with them – the money that Sahab had arranged for the admission deposit for their university.

The brothers knew that the hotel had a casino. Having never been to one, they decided to give it a go. The two boys got ready in their finest suits and went down for a night of harmless fun. Unfortunately, there was a minimum buy-in, and in a game of roulette, Aslam bhai and Ahsan bhai lost all their money. By the time they got back on the flight, they had absolutely no money to survive in the United States.

While narrating the story later, Ahsan bhai comically poked Aslam bhai and quipped, "You were the one who spent all the money. I got yelled at for no fault of mine."

Aslam bhai looked at his brother and smirked.

"Stop interrupting. You know it was your fault. Let me finish."

The two brothers, ashamed at what they had done, made an SOS call to Dilip Sahab. It wasn't surprising that Dilip Sahab lost his cool. The two boys were given an earful for their irresponsible behaviour, but Sahab immediately got on to the task of figuring out how to send them more money.

Dilip Sahab called someone, who called someone else, who called someone in turn, who called someone, and finally the two brothers had the money in their pockets. It was an exhausting and stressful period for Sahab.

I was in splits by the time they completed their story. I could picture Dilip Sahab angry at the boys, yelling at them.

Aslam bhai's roommate at the university was Nusli Wadia, the billionaire businessman and the chairman of Wadia Group. The brothers lived a good student life in the US.

Despite the ups and downs, Dilip Sahab never shirked his responsibilities towards his family. "When I realized I had to act in movies, I froze. My mind couldn't fathom the repercussions this would have at home. The only reason I took it up was because of the handsome salary. It was too good to be true, and it was too good to pass up. Whenever I thought of the money, I could see the family kitchen running properly, food on the table, new clothes and, above all, less stress for Amma and Aghaji."

Oftentimes the family would visit Deolali, which was their home for a few years in the 1930s. Noor bhai, Sahab's elder brother, settled there permanently, but the rest relocated to Bombay. Even after their relocation, the siblings, especially Ahsan bhai, loved to visit Deolali to enjoy the orchards, the gardens and the country life. He was quite young when they were at Deolali, and that home is where he grew up. Ahsan bhai would never miss an opportunity to revisit his childhood. Their home in Deolali was the one true inheritance they had received from their father.

Sahab did not go there as often as the others.

"Didn't you want to visit your Deolali home?" I asked him once.

"No, I didn't."

"Why not? I thought you loved the countryside."

"I did, which is why I didn't want to go back."

I was confused. I waited and hoped Sahab would follow that statement up with an explanation, but he did not. After waiting for ten minutes, I decided to ask him.

"Deolali is where my mother recuperated. Even my brother. It has a lot of memories. A lot of beautiful memories. I don't think I will be able to visit the place without getting emotional."

"Sahab, I hope you don't mind me asking, but aren't the good memories the reason you would want to visit Deolali again?"

Sahab had a faraway look in his eyes. He seemed to have gone back to his childhood – a little boy again, playing among the greenery, running to his mother.

"Some memories are too sweet to visit again. My parents, my childhood, and a lot of memories are attached to Peshawar and Deolali."

I looked at Sahab. I realized he missed his parents, and his home, and he lived with the bittersweet memories of both.

Sakina Aapa, the eldest of all the children, loved and supported Dilip Sahab and the rest like they were her own children. She never married because she knew she had to take care of her family and believed she wouldn't be able to do so if she was responsible for someone else first.

When Dilip Sahab's father had threatened to throw him out of the house, his mother and Sakina Aapa had intervened. As an elder sister, she had pleaded on behalf of her brother. She believed in him and knew he wouldn't do anything that would bring shame and disrespect to his family. So, she advocated for him.

Sakina Aapa made Dilip Sahab assure her that he would consider this job just that, a job.

"Yusuf, you must swear that you will never get lost in that world. You will always remain our Yusuf. You will never embarrass yourself or your family."

And she made sure he kept this promise.

Even after all the years that he spent as an accomplished actor, Dilip Sahab was not allowed to come back home late.

If he did, there were standing instructions from Sakina Aapa that he would have to spend the night in the little outhouse at 48 Pali Hill.

The outhouse was a modest room, about ten-by-ten feet. It had a small bed and was like a modern-day watchman's cabin. That's where Sahab used to sleep if he ever came home late from a shoot, which was quite often – at least until the late 1950s.

"I spent countless nights in that room. It was hilarious how strict Sakina Aapa had always been. I would never miss my grandmother, because Sakina Aapa was always around to remind us of her."

Even though it was Sahab's home, his sister called the shots. She set the basic rules and everyone had to adhere to them.

15

Of Friends and Films

It was January 2004. There was a chill in the air. It was quite cold by Bombay standards. We were at Sahab's home, lounging on the terrace with the eighty-one-year-old icon, who sat there, smiling, a shawl loosely draped shawl over his shoulders. His eyes were closed and his head was tilted back, as if he was trying to soak up the last of the sun's rays.

We were talking about films, something we seldom discussed, despite Dilip Sahab being an actor by profession. We were discussing the good, the bad, the new, the old. And who better to discuss films with than Dilip Sahab, a thespian who had been part of the industry for decades.

"Sahab, have you watched any of the recent movies? They are completely senseless."

Dilip Sahab remained still. He didn't open his eyes, or move his head, or do anything to indicate he had heard me. He usually avoided talking about movies. He used to say, "That's my job. Do you talk about your work at home?"

I wondered if he had actually heard me, but before I could ask again, Sahab said, "Yes, I've seen some. But the fact that films are not as good as earlier isn't the film-maker's fault. It's the audience's fault. They aren't demanding better movies. The person who's making the movie is making it to earn money. It is the audience's responsibility to accept a movie or reject it."

It made sense. Over the years, film-makers, actors and directors have been making movies of inferior quality, but we have not stopped watching them. The bad films make lots of money at the box office and movies of substance get left behind due to lack of PR and marketing.

"What do you think is lacking, Sahab?"

I looked at his face. I knew he knew the answer, but he would still think about it for a minute. Every word he uttered was pure gold.

"A good script. That's what's lacking."

I pondered on that for about a minute. Surprisingly, Sahab followed up with an explanation without me asking for one.

"In any movie, the script is the foundation. That's where it all begins. A producer will pick up a script, or get one written, and then approach artists to enact the characters. There can be a variety of people who work for the movie, but the first step always remains the same. A good script. It's unfortunate that there's such a dearth of good scripts. We don't respect the writers. And what's more unfortunate is that even if there are good writers around, we don't compensate them enough to inspire them. The fact of the matter remains that writers need money too. If we don't pay them, why will they give it their best?"

"That does make sense, Sahab. Whatever field it may be, human resource must be appreciated for the work they put in. They should be rewarded according to what they give. It inspires them to continue giving their best."

"You're right. If the scripts are good, the actors will enjoy reading them too. It will force them to do justice to the characters they have to portray."

"But what about the actors? In some cases, despite the script being good, the actors don't do justice to the characters. What would you suggest they do?"

Sahab smiled. He was enjoying the conversation. He was now looking directly at me. He was thinking, framing the right answer in his head.

"The first rule of good acting is that you can never imagine yourself to be bigger than the character you're playing. I have often said this to people. When you have a script in front of you, it is important to understand the character, and *become* the character."

"And that's what you do?"

"Yes, it is. It's why I faced that bout of depression in my initial years. I became the character I was playing and when my character suffered, I suffered."

"That must have been difficult for you, mentally and emotionally."

"It was. It took a lot of hard work to come out of that dark phase. I would come back home after a long day of shoot. The character who was to die would still be in my mind. Escaping it became more and more difficult. If it wasn't for the doctors in London, it would have been very difficult for me to come out of it."

Before the conversation turned grim, I decided to switch.

"Sahab, what else would you suggest the actors and directors do, to do justice to the script?"

Dilip Sahab smiled again. He realized what I was trying to do and without any hesitation, he went along with the conversation. He and I both didn't want the evening to turn grim.

"Interaction with the crew. It's important to talk to the people on set. They might not have the highest-paying jobs, but they are a part of the team. It is important to speak to them and get to know them. Give time to the post-production team if they request for it. Give a little extra time. The film-makers won't regret it."

"I don't know how the actors today manage this. They are off doing so many projects at the same time. I'm sure there's hardly any time left for interacting with anyone on set. It is my belief that a good actor will never do more than one or two movies at a time. It's not possible to focus and embrace so many characters at the same time. You can't do justice to the characters. You take your work as an example. Will you be able to do justice to your projects if you take up too many at a time?"

"No. Not at all. I will ruin all of them."

"It's the same concept."

I looked at Sahab and realized how much of his work ethic was rooted in common sense and logic. Our industries were poles apart, but his attitude was universal. It would work perfectly even for a CEO of an MNC.

"Sahab, what's the most difficult character you have ever played?"

Sahab smiled. I knew this smile. It meant he wasn't going to answer the question. Maybe too many people had already asked him this.

"Which roles did you enjoy the most?"

Now Sahab chuckled. He knew I wasn't going to let it go.

"I liked all the roles I have played. I signed up for a movie only if I loved the character. In hindsight, I took roles early on in my career that other actors would probably have taken up later in their career, as they dealt with emotionally sensitive topics. They would have taken up such roles after they were well-established in the industry. I, on the other hand, took such roles from the very beginning. I don't know if it was my fortune or my misfortune that I got such roles from the very get-go."

"What about the industry? People must have been offering you only those kinds of roles?"

"Yes, they did. Guru Dutt had approached me once. He had a script and he wanted me to act in the lead role in it."

He continued as I looked at him intently.

"It was another depressing story. I had to refuse. I didn't have any other option."

"Which movie was this?"

Dilip Sahab looked at me and said, "*Pyaasa*."

Aslam bhai once told me that Sahab was approached multiple times by producers in Hollywood. It is widely known that the famous director David Lean was working on a movie based on the life of T.E. Lawrence, a soldier who was renowned for his bravery in World War I. The movie had a character, the role of Sherif Ali, which Lean wanted Dilip Sahab to play. David Lean admired Dilip Sahab and had watched many of his movies and truly believed that no one could play the character of Ali better than Sahab. He stayed at Sahab's house for weeks and tried to convince him to agree to do the film.

Sahab refused. The role eventually went to the actor Omar Sharif, who became a worldwide sensation after the movie's release.

"Sahab, it was such a great opportunity. Why did you turn it down?"

"Why be a small fish in a big pond, when you can be a big fish in a small pond," was his prompt reply. Sahab smiled and looked at me.

"But don't you ever regret it?"

"Every action I take, I do so after putting in a lot of thought into it. I don't regret my decisions. Besides, why do you think that *Lawrence of Arabia* would have been successful if I had been part of it?"

*

I got the opportunity to watch a few movies in the company of Dilip Kumar. He would watch the movies and then give me a review in one sentence. It was always brutally honest and thoroughly enjoyable.

One of the movies we watched together and he truly liked was *Black*, and he had voiced it, often and openly. I asked him his thoughts about *Jodha Akbar*, another movie we watched together at a special screening arranged for Sahab. I wanted to know what he thought of Hrithik Roshan portraying the strong and powerful Emperor Akbar. The last time Dilip Sahab had seen someone play the emperor was in the 1950s when Prithviraj Kapoor played Akbar, the villain in Salim and Anarkali's love story, his hit, *Mughal-E-Azam*.

"The movie is beautiful but they made one mistake. They have made such a powerful emperor so small in character," he said.

In 2002, the new *Devdas* was released. It was a remake of Dilip Sahab's movie of the same name, based on the classic novel by Saratchandra Chatterjee. Shah Rukh Khan had reprised Dilip Sahab's role in the movie, which also starred Aishwarya Rai and Madhuri Dixit. I wanted to know Dilip Sahab's thoughts on the film, which was just about to be released.

We were sitting at Jogger's Park and it was around 10 p.m., when I broached the topic.

"Sahab, do you like Shah Rukh Khan?"

"He's a bright boy. Talks a lot. Why, what happened to him?"

"What do you think of his portrayal of *Devdas*?"

"I'm sure it's a good film. I haven't watched it yet. He's arranging a private screening for me."

He stopped walking as he said this. I could tell he was going back in time. After a brief moment, Sahab resumed walking.

"I remember *Devdas* quite well, as if I finished the shoot yesterday. The most difficult scene I had to shoot was when Devdas learns about his father's demise."

For the next ten minutes, Dilip Sahab enacted the scene in front of me, complete with the dialogues and the emotion. I had not seen *Devdas*. But I was witness to a scene from the movie only a few had seen. I wish we had smartphone cameras then, I could've captured that priceless moment.

I personally like Shah Rukh Khan's work. I've watched a few of his movies and it thrilled me to watch Sanjay Leela Bhansali's version of *Devdas* a few weeks after that night at Jogger's Park. Being one of Sahab's initial hits, there was a lot of pressure on the new *Devdas*, but they did justice to Dilip Sahab's classic.

Dilip Sahab's first memory of Shah Rukh Khan was when he came to Sahab's bungalow one day, as an enthusiastic newcomer in the film industry. He wanted to audition for a movie that Dilip Sahab was planning to make. It was the early 1990s and the movie was titled *Kalinga*. If Shah Rukh Khan had been selected as the lead, it would have been his first, but Sahab had chosen an upcoming talent, Amitosh Maan, instead. Unfortunately, due to some constraints, the movie didn't see the light of day.

However, the persistent and hardworking Shah Rukh Khan remained in touch with Sahab. He became a close acquaintance of Dilip Sahab's family and never missed an opportunity to seek *dua* (blessings) from Sahab and Saira baji. He often visited them and regarded Sahab as his father figure in the film industry.

*

Dilip Kumar had given his all to the film industry, and the film industry had given him so much more in return. It had given him lifelong friends, whom Sahab always cherished. One of his first friends in the film industry was Ashok Kumar, the superstar who had always motivated Sahab.

One evening at his home, over a cup of tea, I asked Sahab who he looked up to the most in the film industry.

"I owe a lot to Ashok bhaiya. I met him on my very first day on set. He gave me an advice I never forgot. He told me that when I act, I should imagine myself in that situation and then find out what my reaction would be to that situation. That would be the acting that'll win hearts and it indeed did."

When two of Dilip Sahab's initial films failed at the box office, Ashok Kumar played a huge role in motivating him. His frequent interactions with the senior actor, their everlasting friendship and his words of wisdom motivated Sahab not to be dejected at the initial setbacks. Ashok Kumar's encouragement and endorsement of Yusuf Khan's efforts, and guidance to come up with his own nuances of acting helped Dilip Kumar improve his craft.

"Another major influence in my career was S. Mukherjee sahab. He was an institution in himself. I'll never forget his emphasis on physical fitness for actors, his paternal-style guidance and his endearing attitude towards me. I don't know why, but he always had a lot of appreciation for my work. He would often call me and I would humbly appreciate his critical feedback and admiration."

Dilip Sahab truly enjoyed the work of a few international stars as well. He was a big fan of Ingrid Bergman and when her latest film hit the theatres, the young Dilip Kumar made sure he watched it many times. He was so impressed and mesmerized by the classic *For Whom the Bells Tolls* (1943), starring Ingrid

Bergman and Gary Cooper, that he watched it twenty-one times over three days!

Another international star Sahab loved was James Stewart.

Conversing with Sahab, I had once asked him, "People speak so highly about your talent. What movie of yours would you recommend to budding actors so they can learn from your acting?"

Sahab smiled at me. What he said made me respect him more.

"I have always been a hardworking actor. I try and keep learning and improving, but I'm far from being the best. If you must watch a film, watch *Harvey*, an exceptional movie starring James Stewart. It taught me that the one thing you must do is make sure your emotions are not only reflected in your body language, but also in your eyes."

Dilip Sahab had reached out to James Stewart in the 1960s and also shortly before his unfortunate demise. He mentioned to me how he was invited to London to watch *Harvey* on stage, performed by Stewart in the 1960s. He was in awe of the powerful and impactful performance by everyone on stage and the tears everyone in the audience had shed. It was even more special because the Queen of England was present there as well.

"This industry is so difficult. There's someone younger and incredibly talented coming in every day. Did you ever compare yourself to them?" I had asked him once.

"I just did my work. Whenever I compared my acting skills with other actors, I always found that I had a lot to learn. I never got envious. They were simply doing their job and I was doing mine."

As Sahab looked at me, I knew he had more to say.

"I sometimes think it's so strange that I, of all people, became an actor. Can you imagine a fruit merchant's son, a Pathan's son becoming an actor?"

"That's the result of your hard work and dedication."

"That's not always enough. Sometimes, fate has a little something to do with it. For me, acting was a job. It was never a channel to achieve celebrity status. I wanted to put food on the table and a roof over my family's head. When I was young, I would think of the agony I faced due to separation from friends and family from Peshawar and how circumstances brought me into this world. The experience of the Partition hurts me even today. But I think this is what the Almighty had in mind for me."

As he finished, Dilip Sahab quoted a verse from the Quran, Chapter 6, Verse 59, for me. "And with Him are the keys of the unseen; none knows them except Him. And He knows what is on the land and in the sea. Not a leaf falls but that He knows it. And no grain is there within the darkness of the earth and no moist or dry [thing] but that it is [written] in a clear record."

Another close and dear friend of Sahab was the iconic actor Pran Krishan Sikand, popularly known as Pran. He was dubbed the villain of the millennium by *Stardust* magazine.

Even after their retirement from the film industry, they would constantly be in touch with each other. I have watched Sahab, on various occasions, chatting with Pran Sahab over the phone. Their light conversations in Punjabi always left Sahab smiling.

Once, when I heard the news about his Pran Sahab's poor health, I asked Sahab if he was going to meet him. "No question about it. If I don't go meet him, who will," he had said.

Sahab had once told me, "Pran would play negative characters flawlessly, but there is no bigger gentleman than him. I have never witnessed him out of line with anyone, in any scenario. India's most famous bad guy had a spotless reputation. He used to tell me wherever in the world he is, he would make it to my wedding."

The world knows that he did. Despite the terrible weather conditions in Srinagar, where Pran Sahab had been shooting at the time of Dilip Sahab's marriage, he had caught a flight, braved the turbulence and made it to his dear friend's wedding.

"I didn't think he would be able to come. Saira and I had announced our wedding at a very short notice. We didn't have time to invite anyone properly. He still came."

After Pran Sahab's demise, Dilip Sahab told me that the only thing that upset him was that his dear friend wasn't considered for the Dadasaheb Phalke award sooner. He was a great actor and a deserving candidate. He should have been graced with the award years before he actually received it.

Although I met a few of Sahab's friends at his house, the only friend whose home I visited with him was Naushad Sahab's. Naushad Ali was one of the most popular music composers in India. With a career that spanned over sixty years, Naushad Sahab's music has been one of the most celebrated in the Indian film industry. I consider myself lucky to have had the privilege of sharing a cup of tea with him at his home.

There were quite a few occasions when Dilip Sahab had asked me to accompany him to Naushad Sahab's home. We would go to his home during late afternoons or early evenings, right on time for tea. It was one of the few places where Dilip Sahab was addressed by his real name. To the kids at Naushad Sahab's place, he was Yusuf uncle.

Naushad Sahab's family loved Dilip Sahab. Naushad Sahab owned a villa facing the Carter Road seaside in Bandra, named 'Ashiyana'. During Dilip Sahab's visits, the two legends would sit in the large living room, enjoying each other's company in silence. In the hours that I spent with them, both men used to speak only for ten or fifteen minutes, remaining quiet the rest of the time.

Initially, I did not mind the silence. Eventually though, it would become slightly awkward, as I realized that I could not scroll through my phone while sitting with them, as that would appear rude. So one day, after about fifteen minutes of silence, I decided it was time to break the silence. It was too quiet for a Saturday afternoon.

"I watched *Mughal-E-Azam* last night," I said, referring to the Dilip Kumar starrer for which Naushad Sahab was the music composer.

"Were you watching it for the first time?" Naushad Sahab asked.

"No, uncle. I watched it for the tenth time yesterday. It is my favourite movie. I love its songs."

Dilip Sahab smiled. He looked happy and there was also a hint of pride in his expression.

He said, "See, Naushad Sahab, even the youngsters enjoy the movie and its songs."

Naushad Sahab beamed.

"My favourite songs are *Pyaar Kiya Toh Darna Kya* and *Teri Mehfil Mein Qismat*," I said.

"When I first received the lyrics for *Pyaar Kiya Toh Darna Kya*, Dilip Sahab, K. Asif Sahab (the director of *Mughal-E-Azam*), Lata (Mangeshkar) and I were sitting right here in this room. When I played the tune on my grand piano, Lata jumped with joy. She insisted that we record the song right away. Dilip Sahab had asked her to be patient," Naushad sahab said.

Dilip Sahab and Naushad Sahab burst into laughter. Continuing the tale of this legendary song, Naushad Sahab told me about the night before they were to record.

"We spent the entire night on the terrace of this very house. Shakeel Badayuni (the lyricist) and I worked hard the entire night. By the time we perfected the song, it was morning."

This was something I hadn't known.

"The entire night? Was it a very difficult song?" I asked.

Naushad Sahab smiled. He seemed to be enjoying the conversation.

"It was difficult. But we wanted to make sure that there wasn't any trouble during the recording."

"What kind of trouble?"

"I know Lata well. I understand her voice. I know what suits her voice. I wanted to make sure that enunciating the words did not hinder Lata's singing in any way."

Lata Mangeshkar, or Lata didi, is a phenomenon. She has sung thousands of songs in her life and continues to inspire new artists every day. She started her career as a child artist in movies, singing songs in Marathi, eventually moving to Bombay to work in Hindi cinema. During her initial years in the industry, only a handful of people believed in her, which included Naushad Sahab. Most preferred a deep baritone like that of Shamshad Begum over Lata didi's shriller voice.

Eventually, Lata Mangeshkar found the appreciation she deserved. In those days most songs were written in Urdu. Initially, Lata Mangeshkar found it tough to enunciate some of the Urdu words. There was a hint of Marathi accent in her enunciation. Dilip Sahab realized Lata Mangeshkar's talents and her potential and he wanted her to work hard to become successful. To help push her forward, Sahab suggested improving her Urdu diction. Hard working and determined, she took Urdu lessons to improve her hold over the language. Eventually, she became a superstar.

Lata Mangeshkar loved Dilip Sahab and considered him as her elder brother. She would lovingly call him 'Yusuf bhai'. She had sung several songs in Dilip Sahab's movies and often sang on numbers picturized on Saira Banu. In an interview, she had even claimed that she believed 'her voice best suited the beautiful actress, Saira Banu, the loving wife of Dilip Sahab. They are family.'

The few times that I heard him on the phone with her, he would lovingly call her '*meri pyari behen*' (my sweet sister). She would often visit Sahab, especially on Raksha Bandhan. I was a witness to their familial affection for each other when she visited Sahab few years ago.

The conversation around *Mughal-E-Azam* continued.

Dilip Sahab had once mentioned to me that Shapoorji Pallonji, owner of the Shapoorji Pallonji Group, and the financier of *Mughal-E-Azam*, was a big fan of Dilip Kumar and loved the character of Akbar. Whenever the movie's budget would run low, K. Asif would invite Mr Shapoorji to watch scenes that depicted Emperor Akbar in all his glory. When Shapoorji would be ready to leave the set, K. Asif would politely inform him about the financial crunch and request for more money to keep the production running.

On one such day, when K. Asif asked Mr Shapoorji for additional finances, the multi-millionaire turned to the director and in his typical Gujarati-Parsi dialect, said, *"Tameh picture banao chhe, ya maro makbaro banao chhe?"* (Are you making a movie, or are you making my tomb?)

The two fell silent for a minute, then burst into laughter.

Another woman Sahab appreciated for her hard work was Nalini Jaywant. Although she had a relatively short stint in the film industry, her attitude towards work on set inspired many.

Dilip Sahab's admiration and affection for Noor Jehan was also well known. An accomplished singer, actor and a beauty queen, she was adored by millions. She started her career in 1935. She was given the title of *'Malika-E-Tarannum'*, which translates to Queen of Melody, and was later referred to as Madam Noor Jehan, or simply as 'Madam'.

Noor Jehan's husband, Shaukat Hussain Rizvi, originally from Azamgarh, Uttar Pradesh (incidentally the town my ancestors hail from), was a producer and director and produced Sahab's first blockbuster movie *Jugnu*, in 1947. Unfortunately, later in the same year, after the Partition, Shaukat Hussain Rizvi decided to move to Pakistan. His wife, Noor Jehan, followed. There, she acted in hundreds of movies and sang thousands of ghazals and songs. Her contribution to the Pakistani film and music world is unparalleled. Despite the troubled relationship between India and Pakistan, she was, like many other artists, a bridge between the two countries.

When Noor Jehan and her husband moved to Pakistan, Sahab felt the loss. He once described to me how her renditions of some of Faiz Ahmad Faiz's ghazals conveyed so much pain. "When Shaukat Sahab and Noor Jehan left, I realized what it meant to lose friends."

Thirty-five years after the Partition, they met again. During the Golden Jubilee celebration of the Indian talkie, Noor Jehan was invited to India. The entire country was overjoyed when she said 'yes' to the invitation. Sahab could not have been happier. He briefly narrated to me the moment he met Noor Jehan again in 1982, and how he had welcomed her to India, at a concert in her honour at Bombay's Shanmukhananda Hall.

"I still remember that one line I had said to her. It came straight from my heart."

"What did you say?"

"*Noor Jehan-ji, jitne baras aap humse door raheen, theek utne hi baras humne aapka intezaar kiya.*" (Noor Jehan, we waited for you all the years you stayed away from us.)

*

I loved talking to Sahab about his friends. He would get nostalgic while talking about them. He would often enjoy telling me about his close friend and actor, Baldev.

Baldev, popularly known as Sunil Dutt, started his career on the radio as a journalist. He had migrated from Pakistan after the Partition and after a lot of hard work and struggle, earned a job at All-India Radio. Dilip Sahab had already become an established actor by then.

During the early 1950s, as an editor for All-India Radio, Baldev was given the task of interviewing as many movie celebrities as he could. Dilip Kumar was obviously on the top of his list. He hadn't succeeded in interviewing Dilip Sahab despite multiple attempts.

One evening, though, his life changed. Baldev received information that Dilip Kumar would be at a particular location in Khandala for a shoot and would be accessible for a few days. Not wanting to waste any time, he immediately headed for Khandala, which is a few hours from Mumbai.

Dilip Kumar was impressed with the dedication and determination the young man displayed. A few years later, when he was launched as an actor, they became close friends. Baldev even bought a house next to Sahab on Pali Hill. Sahab always referred to Sunil Dutt as 'Baldev'.

Amitabh Bachchan once narrated an incident when he called up Sahab, requesting to meet late at night, and Sahab, in his jovial tone, had smiled and said, "Yes, please come."

Amitabh Bachchan, as a part of his contribution to Dilip Kumar's autobiography *The Substance and the Shadow*, wrote, "The history of Indian cinema shall in my reckoning be 'before Dilip sahab' and 'after Dilip sahab', because of his impeccable presence."

In one of his famous blog posts, he wished Dilip Sahab on his birthday, putting forward his views on what he thought of the man. Dilip Sahab, forever the gentleman, wasted no time in dictating a letter and responding to him. I remember that day when Saira baji and I informed Sahab about Amitabh Bachchan's blog.

It was a cold morning. I had just woken up. I groggily reached for my phone and rubbed my eyes to focus on the small Apple iPhone screen. The date flashed on its lock screen: 11 December, Dilip Sahab's birthday.

As a force of habit, I started browsing on the phone to check the latest news updates of the day.

The Internet was full of birthday wishes for Dilip Sahab. I also noticed a Twitter notification mentioning Dilip Kumar. I clicked on it and was redirected to Amitabh Bachchan's blog. Late at night, the Bollywood superstar Amitabh Bachchan had written a letter to his idol. He had wished him on his birthday, reminiscing about the old times when they had worked together. I couldn't wait to show this to Sahab.

I got ready quickly and left for Dilip Sahab's house. I didn't know if he had read it yet, but I had to speak to him about it. As I entered his home, the morning sun had just started to radiate its heat but the air was still chilly.

I entered Sahab's home, ready to break the news to him, when I saw Saira baji sitting on a wooden chair facing the lawn, looking at a sheet in one hand, gently wiping away a tear with the other. I walked towards her. She turned to me when she heard footsteps approaching her.

She smiled at me and held up the sheet for me to see. It was a printout of the blog I had read earlier. Amitabh Bachchan's words had left me speechless, and they had overwhelmed Saira baji. I smiled at her and she knew I had already read it. She simply got up from the chair and together, we headed for the second floor to Dilip Sahab. We had to show him the beautiful letter.

Sahab was just finishing his morning ablutions. He was settling down on the beige leather couch, with a bunch of newspapers and a pen.

Saira baji and I walked towards him with huge smiles on our faces. Sahab, with a pair of glasses perched on his nose, looked up to see us approaching him. He noticed my smile and smiled back and then looked at his wife's face. His smile faded and a look of confusion replaced it. He noticed the sheet in Saira baji's hands. She reached her husband, smiled, and handed the printout to him. He read it once, and then again.

We both sat beside him, patiently waiting for a response. His smile spoke more eloquently than he probably ever could. I could see happiness, pride, humility, and tears.

Sahab looked at Saira, and without words, they exchanged their joy at the letter. Sahab then turned his gaze to me.

"I cannot believe how beautifully he has written this. It's one of the best birthday gifts one could have ever asked for. Would you write my reply to him? I will dictate it to you."

I whipped out my smartphone and opened the notepad. I was ready.

Once we were done, Uday Narayan Tara (Sahab's close family friend and an accomplished journalist who helped complete Sahab's autobiography) was asked to edit the reply. Then I read it out aloud to him, he made some changes, and I offered to post this response on Sahab's blog (which I was asked to set up within a few hours). And so Dilip Kumar thanked Amitabh Bachchan for so eloquently wishing him on his birthday.

The blogs are still posted online. All you have to do is Google them.

Amitabh Bachchan's blog (Day 1331; Dated 10 December, 2011; Mumbai)

It's a celebration for the greatest, on the eve of his birthday. He will turn 89 tomorrow, the 11th of December. Exactly 20 years older to me by birth and exactly 2000 years ahead of me in our common vocation. He is my idol and has been since the day I first saw his work. He has been an inspiration not just for me but I am certain to thousands of those that have ever dreamt of facing a camera for the art form called cinema. His presence, his aura and his dedication to film shall be documented as 'before Dilip Kumar and after Dilip Kumar'. He set fresh norms of performance in his acts of excellence, faultless and beyond any kind of improvement. His greatest quality was his connect with those that stood before him in the frame to act. His strength of delivery and his strength of connect with any character he portrayed have been unique and unsurpassable. On the eve of his birthday, I wish him good health and a long life of peace and happiness. He was the best and still is. Dilip Kumar, Yusuf Khan, Dilip Saheb … happy birthday!!

I entered his spacious home after decades. After minor cosmetic changes, it has remained the same. My visits to his place have been limited, but eventful on each occasion. A meeting of the artists and the film fraternity, a midnight informal call, a casual trip to see his excellent skills at badminton, or a shoot at his luxurious lawns during the making of Zameer with his wife and my co-star Saira ji, Saira Banu! All have been clearly etched in my mind. And why not? He was the one actor that we as young students in University broke boundaries and hostel rules to go see his films night after night. His early films had been historic in content and repute – Aan and Shaheed – ones that I still remember seeing in the darkness of cinema halls with the barest minimum facility and comfort. For 4 annas, 25 paise, a quarter of a rupee, we would sit on wooden benches right up in front in the theatres and marvel at what our hero would enact. And among the many that we saw and enjoyed, it was for me always a Dilip Kumar that stood out. Different and distinguished. And always without fault.

And then one day I stood along with him on the sands of Juhu as the camera rolled to give the mahurat shot for Shakti, the only film that we worked together in. Our first shooting scene in the film was in a jail sequence, where the police official but also my Father in the film comes to visit me and tries to convince me that I was taking a wrong path in life and I disagree. Tough to stand in front of one whom you have admired for ages, and disagree with. But it happened and it kept happening day after day, till the film was complete. There were electric moments between him and me in the script, written by that incredible team of writers Salim-Javed, and each moment was filled with the distinction of great and impressive drama.

The film completed its work during the same time when I was injured during Coolie and released when I was still recovering from my ailment. The final print was shown to me on a makeshift theatre put up in Prateeksha, for I was still not well enough to move out of the house. Did I ever imagine many years ago, as I sat in a rather ill-equipped theatre in a corner of Kathmandu in Nepal, around 1954, that I would one day share the same screen space with this tremendous talent that would explode in front of me. Never! And it still remains an illusion in my life to have actually been a part of a project which was headed by this thespian! God has been kind, very kind!!

Good night and may you always be blessed …

Dilip Sahab's response (personal blog; dated 14 December 2011; Mumbai)

My Dear Amitabh:

With tears of pride in her eyes Saira handed over the printout of your eloquent tribute to my work in your blog. I read it once, then again and again.

As you yourself would be keenly aware, we actors are completely oblivious of ourselves and our surroundings while we perform and, even when we watch our work in the rushes shown to us, our senses and vision are trained to detect shortcomings more than accomplishments. That's the only way we know to improve and render performances that come close to our own satisfaction. And it is always the audience who have the absolute right to acclaim or reject our work, however hard we may have worked to achieve perfection and excellence.

I am certainly privileged to know from your affectionate compliments that someone as knowledgeable and competent as you has liked my work. Yes, now that you have reminded me, I can recall the scenes that brought us together before the cameras for Shakti. I should say the respect and admiration are mutual. Not just Shakti, your work in several films I have watched has been world class and inimitable. In recent times I can remember Black and, if I remember right, Saira and I were at a loss for words at the premiere night, after the curtain came down, to express our myriad feelings of admiration for your outstanding performance. It is a pity the film missed the Oscar nomination. If any Indian actor, in my personal opinion, deserves the world's most coveted award, it is you. I have heard so much about Paa which we didn't catch up with. You know how Saira is – she never could see me die in my films and she could not muster the courage to see your death scene in Paa.

Thank you, Amitabh, for your warm love and good wishes. May God keep you, Jaya and your family happy always.

DK

16

A Little Misunderstanding

Pali Hill is an upmarket residential area in Bandra West, Mumbai. If you take a stroll there, you are quite likely to bump into a movie star or a celebrity. Originally an affluent, British officers' residential enclave, Pali Hill started attracting Indians in the early 1930s, when a few magazine and newspaper owners, fell in love with the view and purchased land in the area to build their dream homes. Back then, most of Pali Hill was under forest cover. The sea was visible from the peaks of the western side of the hill. Initially, there were only bungalows and villas dotting the area. In the early 1960s, the first high-rises came up in the area and soon, many others followed. Although a majority of the people were still living in bungalows, many of them slowly started selling their homes to real estate developers for generous profits.

In the 1940s, Dilip Sahab frequented Bandra's seaside for picnics with the family. What is now known as Carter Road was then a piece of uninhabited seafront with coconut groves and tamarind trees, perfect for day-long retreat with family and friends.

Around 1947, Dilip Sahab and his family used to stay at a small but cosy rented house on Pali Mala Road, next to the present-day Sunrise Restaurant. By 1952, he had become quite successful and purchased a villa on Pali Hill. It was an ideal place for his ailing mother and aging father, given the pure non-polluted breeze and the greenery in the posh neighbourhood.

Dilip Sahab's villa, 48 Pali Hill, resembled a French chateau and was built on half an acre of land. Once the family moved in, they spent a fortune fixing it and making it their own.

We used to stay at our house in Pali Village, which was a few minutes away from Pali Hill. Coincidentally, our address was 48 Pali Village, and Dilip Sahab's was 48 Pali Hill. It was almost as if we were meant to cross paths.

For Dilip Sahab, the Pali Hill bungalow was the place where he felt the most peaceful and comfortable. Most of his work would be in the studios situated in the Goregaon-Malad area, which was closer to Pali Hill.

As the years passed, more and more people from the film industry started purchasing homes in Pali Hill. Immediately after Sahab, his close friend Naushad Sahab bought a bungalow on the other side of Pali Hill, on the sea-facing Carter Road. Much later, Naseem Banu, Dilip Sahab's mother-in-law, on her son Sultan's insistence, also bought two acres of land in Pali Hill. The area was too sombre for her liking, but she had eventually given in to her son's persistence.

Naseem Banu built a spacious bungalow on this plot. Now known as 34/B Pali Hill, it is a stone's throw away from Dilip Sahab's 48 Pali Hill. Eventually, a few years after their marriage, Sahab and Saira baji moved into Naseem Banu's home. When Sahab and Saira baji were still living at 48 Pali Hill, Naseem

Banu would often encourage them to hold their meetings and soirees at her home instead, as there were fewer people and hence, less distraction.

I have had so many of my conversations with Sahab on the terrace of the two-storey bungalow at 34/B Pali Hill. The entrance to this old property had a huge black metal gate, with guards posted outside. It still looks slightly intimidating.

The gate opens up to a steep upward slope that leads to a multistorey building on the left and Naseem Banu's three-storey home in the centre of the plot. It is old, and except for a few pieces of furniture here and there, it has not seen much modification in a long time.

The ground floor opens to a large foyer and to its right is a vast living room where Sahab would usually meet his acquaintances. A huge portrait of Dilip Sahab and Saira baji adorns one of the walls. The rest of the ground floor includes a room for Sahab's office staff, the kitchen, and living quarters for the helpers. A staircase and a lift connect the ground floor to the other floors.

The first floor has two large bedrooms with antique wardrobes and trunks. The furniture carved in wood and metal looks old, but grand. Naseem Banu and her mother Shamshad Begum (Saira Banu's grandmother) lived on one side of that floor, while Sahab and Saira baji lived on the other side. Sahab eventually moved to the third floor once it was renovated.

Once, when Saira baji was accompanying me down the stairs, one of the old trunks piqued my curiosity and I asked her what was in it. It seemed to hold some long-forgotten secrets and treasures from the past. Saira baji simply smiled at me. She had a cheeky grin on her face and a twinkle in her eyes.

"It has the evidence of my romance with the world's greatest lover," she said.

In those trunks, Saira baji had stored each one of the letters and photos Sahab had shared with her. There were handwritten letters with the promise of tomorrow and the declaration of love, there were countless photos that Dilip Sahab and Saira baji had clicked over the years.

Frankly, the décor of the first two floors is slightly outdated for my liking. I find it rather gloomy, especially when compared to the comfort, warmth and cosiness of the third floor. I usually went straight to the third floor, which was Sahab's living space for years.

The third floor has a beautiful terrace, a spacious living room and a bedroom. The spotless floor also has a high ceiling, which adds to its grandeur. My favourite place to sit was beside Sahab's recliner on the beige leather sofa.

During the months preceding Naseem Banu's death, she was quite ill and in a lot of pain. Once, while at Jogger's Park, Sahab told me, "I cannot bear to see her in pain. She screams all night. Saira is always taking care of her. I pray to Allah Almighty that she recovers soon."

Naseem Banu died in 2002. A year later, on 2 November 2003, her son Sultan Ahmed's wife, Rahat Sultan, also passed away. I can never forget that day. It was the one time I felt that Sahab would never speak to me. I thought I was never going to be invited to his home again.

It was about 9.30 p.m. when we received the call about Rahat Sultan passing away. Asif bhai and I got ready to go to Sahab's house. My elder brother had already spoken to Saira baji and she had told us that Sahab would be waiting at the bungalow, while the mourners would be gathering at Sultan bhai and Rahat Sultan's apartment in their building, which was in the 34/B Pali Hill compound. We had to meet Sahab and escort him to Sultan bhai's apartment.

So, we reached Sahab's place and accompanied him to the apartment complex. Many people had gathered to offer their condolences to the family. The house was full and there was an eerie buzz from the hushed whispers in the apartment.

Inside Sultan bhai's apartment, Sahab held on to Saira baji's hand. The constant wave of people approaching them was starting to make Sahab uneasy. He seemed to be getting overwhelmed by the gathering. Saira baji could feel her husband's discomfort, and within fifteen minutes, looked at me and Asif bhai. She indicated that Sahab needed to be escorted back to the bungalow, and willingly, we obliged.

Being diabetic, Dilip Sahab had to be particular about when he took his meals and medicines. By the time we reached his home, it was well beyond his usual mealtime. A house help had set up his dinner as per Saira baji's instructions. But Sahab insisted on eating only when Saira baji was back.

"Sahab, Saira ma'am will take time. She told us that we should get your food ready. Can I please bring out the plates for you?" the help insisted.

After a brief pause, Sahab agreed. He also told us to eat with him.

My brother interjected.

"Sahab, we had eaten before we left home. We won't eat but we'll sit with you."

"It's almost midnight. You guys should eat with me."

Eventually, we gave in.

After dinner, Sahab suggested that we spend some time on the porch, as he wanted some fresh air.

From the porch, we could see people still coming and going towards Sultan bhai's apartment. We watched as the mourners headed to the flat, heads bent low, adding to the gloom of the night. People were too distracted to notice the three of us sitting out in the open. The ones who did, politely nodded in our direction and walked away graciously respecting our need for space and privacy.

The silence was deafening and I didn't know how to break it. I looked at my brother, and then at Sahab. I sighed, closed my eyes and tilted my head back. Eventually, it was Dilip Sahab who broke the silence.

"Rahat-ji left us."

I didn't know how to respond to that. As if reading my mind, my brother leaned forward and held Sahab's hand.

Sahab probably didn't want the awkward silence to linger, so he changed the topic and asked, "How have you guys been? What are you up to these days?"

"Sahab, please take care of your health. Eat your meals on time," Asif bhai said.

Dilip Sahab looked at Asif bhai and smiled. He turned to me with the same smile.

I, however, was still thinking about Rahat Sultan leaving us. I wanted to comfort Dilip Sahab as best as I could.

Sahab then spoke about how within the last few years, Saira's grandmother, mother and now bhabhi, Rahat Sultan, left this world so suddenly.

I could see that Asif bhai and Sahab were affected by each other's moods. Asif bhai was more attached to Sahab than anybody else and Sahab was also quite close to him. They were like father and son. Many times, I had felt like an outsider in their midst.

Sahab suddenly looked to me and said, "Faisal, what are you doing tomorrow?"

"Nothing much, Sahab. I'll go to work. The usual."

We went back to silence. I straightened up and positioned my chair closer to Sahab. I leaned towards him and asked,

"Sahab, agar aap bura na maanein to kuch kahoon." ("Sahab, if you don't mind, can I say something?")

"Ji, kahiye. Kya kehna hai?" (Yes, tell me.)

"Sahab, you should do something about your 48 Pali Hill property. Develop it, or sell it. Do whatever you want, but in your lifetime. No one will be able to take care of it after you are gone. And the builder mafia will create problems for everybody."

As soon as I had uttered these words, I saw utter horror on my brother's face. He was shocked. I looked at Dilip Sahab and I could see his face going pale for a moment, before turning red in anger.

He lifted his right hand and pointed one finger at me. In a booming voice, he said, "No such thing will happen! 48 Pali Hill will be just fine."

I could feel my heart racing. I couldn't understand what had happened. As the silence took over, I could hear the faint noise of the insects in the air. It seemed as if it had suddenly turned colder.

I wanted to leave. I was hoping that Sahab would ask me to leave. I was nervous. I was scared. I was ashamed. As luck would have it, Saira baji returned home and we asked Sahab if we could leave now. He dismissed us in a flat and exhausted tone.

On our way back home, Asif bhai confronted me about my audacity.

"Faisal, you should not have spoken to Sahab that way. Even I haven't spoken to him in this manner."

"Asif bhai, I didn't mean any disrespect."

When I asked Sahab to consider his options with the property he owned, the only thought in my head was that he was growing old. He had had a beautiful life, but he didn't have an heir. No sons or daughters to take care of his home after him.

I couldn't understand Dilip Sahab's response that day. Even today, as I think about that night, I don't understand why he had such a strong reaction. It seemed as if he wasn't ready to face the reality of life. As humans, we are an arrogant race. Each one of us pretends to go through life without acknowledging that life, in fact, is short, and very volatile. The one thing we can be assured of is that if there is a high, there will be a low. During our highs we just forget that the low is just around the corner.

I wanted to make sure that he would be able to take care of his home, the place where he lived with his family, the home that had countless memories…

I was concerned from the legal point of view. In a neighbourhood as small as Pali Hill, even though there are thousands of residents, most people know about each other's properties. A few years ago, a long-time resident of Pali Hill passed away. He owned a huge plot and a beautiful bungalow stood elegantly upon it.

After his demise, land sharks forged documents to take over his property. His demise was a painful experience for his family. Not just emotionally, but also financially. I didn't want Dilip Sahab, Saira baji, or any of their family members to face similar difficulties. Life is fickle. No one knows what's going to happen, and land sharks are brutal. They don't care who you are, or what condition you're in. They only care about the money they can make off a property.

I didn't push the conversation with him that night but I heard rumours that Dilip Sahab was planning something with a renowned architect. They were considering a few options for the half-acre 48 Pali Hill property, sitting on prime land.

Unfortunately, Sahab's plans didn't materialize, and a few years later, a man, a prominent real estate developer, notorious for manipulating property records, had forged documents to lay claim to the same property Sahab had dismissed me over. Dilip Sahab had purchased 48 Pali Hill in 1952, and in 2010, this man suddenly claimed that his father had purchased it from the original owners in 1982. He also claimed that Dilip Sahab was just a tenant on the property. After years of struggle, Dilip Sahab and Saira baji were finally able to prove the validity of their rightful ownership of the property and call out the forgery. It was this that I had tried to warn him against.

The years they put into the fight with the scamster made Sahab and Saira baji suffer mentally, physically and emotionally. Dilip Sahab battled not only the scamster, but also the stress-related diseases that followed. Saira baji's brother Sultan aided Sahab in his fight against the scamster. All the stress of the 48 Pali Hill legal battle took a toll on the ever-happy and jovial Sultan bhai, and he died of a sudden stroke in January 2016.

Back then, Asif bhai was sure that after that night, Sahab would never converse with me the way he used to. He was sure that I had crossed a line. Even I had almost thought that this was the last decent conversation I was ever going to have with Dilip Sahab. But I believe that somewhere, he probably realized where I was coming from. A few days later, I joined Sahab on his terrace for snacks, sandwiches and tea. Nothing had changed.

I learnt a very important lesson through these years. A fear that resulted in a small conversation that began on a cold night in 2003 ended with a legal struggle that took years away from the people I love.

No matter how big or small one is, life is cruel. Without children, it's even more so. Despite what happens in life, or what the current reality is, when you have the strength, secure your assets, divide your properties among your next of kin and manage your finances.

Old age is tricky. It comes with a lot of work and weakness. On so many occasions, the mind can't handle the fact that the body is not capable of living the life your mind wants to. My only wish for when I grow old is that I am not dependent on anyone. Watching Dilip Sahab, and even my own mother, battle their age, and the realities of life, has been a humbling experience. I wish no one ever has to face the difficulties that come with old age, but that would mean I am in denial.

Life happens, and so does old age. The best we can do is prepare for the worst, and do right by our children and family.

17

The Foodie

As I have mentioned before, Dilip Kumar was always curious about the simple things in life. One thing that excited his imagination was food. My wife and bhabhis enjoyed discussing different cuisines and recipes with him.

Love for good food ran in his family. Sahab's brothers, Ahsan and Aslam, share the same fondness. When my wife talked about a particular dish, their faces would light up, and the conversation would invariably end with the brothers requesting that we send some of the food over the next time it was prepared.

The two years (1941 to 1943) Yusuf Khan spent in Pune running the army canteen made him fall in love with the kitchen. One of his secret recipes was the 'Dilip Kumar omelette'. It was his own creation and he never ate an omelette unless it was prepared his way.

Sahab and Saira baji personally trained a cook well, to the point that she knew exactly how much salt was to be used in which preparation. She had been around for more than thirty years, preparing their food exactly how they liked it. Sahab had also shared some of his recipes with us. Even today, every time I feel like having a good omelette, it's usually the Dilip Kumar omelette.

In 2004, on a busy late afternoon, while I was swamped with work, I received a call from Sahab.

"Faisal, I have a friend. He has come to Mumbai. He is staying at a hotel here in Juhu. He has come from Nagpur for three-four days for some work. He has invited me for dinner. The problem is that he told me he didn't like the food they serve at his hotel."

"Sahab, would you like to go to some restaurant? There are a lot of good restaurants in Juhu."

"No, we'll eat at his hotel suite. There will be some other people as well. I was wondering whether we can arrange for some food to be delivered to his room."

"Sahab, should I arrange for food from outside?"

"Yes, it'll be great if you could."

"Sahab, how many more people will be there with you?"

Despite a number of people working for him, Dilip Sahab had chosen me for this extremely personal matter. It made me feel important. He trusted my choice and that was the biggest compliment I had ever received in my life. It was also his way of showing his love for me.

"I don't know. There should be about four or five more people. But you can make arrangements for seven to eight people."

Today, there are a number of online food delivery services available, but back then, there were none. Most good restaurants didn't even deliver food. They'd ask you to come and pick your order up. I had to figure out what Sahab would want and then try to find how to get the food delivered.

"Sahab, what would you like to eat?"

"Look, let's order some *paya* soup. Everyone will love it."

I nodded, as I scribbled Sahab's wish-list on a piece of paper on my desk.

"Then let's have some of those long kebabs. What do you call them?"

"Sahab, seekh kebab?"

"Yes, yes. Seekh kebab. Please order some of that."

"Okay, Sahab. I will order that as well."

"Ok, the UP-style korma will be nice too. You know that, right? It has a lot of spices, but less salt."

"Yes, Sahab."

And then there was a long pause. I could hear him thinking, trying to create the best menu for the special dinner.

"We will definitely be having biryani. What do you think?"

"Yes, Sahab, there definitely should be biryani. Will the UP-style biryani be good for you?"

"Yes, that will be good. Please make sure they serve it with some *raita* and onion."

"Yes, Sahab, I'll make sure all that is there."

I was about to hang up, when Sahab started speaking again.

"Don't forget the korma at all."

"Absolutely not, Sahab. I have noted everything down."

"Please also add *bhuna hua keema* (roasted minced meat) and *bheja* (goat's brain)."

My mind was racing. I had absolutely no clue where to find a restaurant that would serve all these dishes, that too prepared well enough for Dilip Sahab to like.

"Excellent. Please add rotis, *pao* and *buroon pao* too, Faisal. It'll be nice to eat with paya soup and korma."

"Ok, sure."

"I hope I mentioned korma?"

I chuckled a little. "Yes, Sahab. You said you want the UP-style korma."

I waited on the line. I could hear Sahab thinking. He was truly enjoying himself. I could sense Sahab relishing my disbelief at the number of items he had listed. While he was trying to figure out what else to order, I was trying to figure out which restaurant to order from. I was also thinking which restaurant could send along some people to serve Sahab and his guests.

As I was about to hang up, Sahab spoke again.

"I completely forgot *raan* (roasted goat's leg). We Pathans love it. It's our favourite."

"Noted. Sahab, when do you want the food to be delivered?"

"Tomorrow evening."

"Ok, Sahab. What time should I send the food?"

"Why, won't you be joining us?"

"Sahab, I will be in Bangalore tomorrow. I'll be back late at night."

"Ok, we will plan a spread like this with you some other time then. For tomorrow, please send the food by 7 p.m. Just tell the guys that we will pay upon delivery."

"Sahab, don't worry about anything, everything will be taken care of."

After discussing two or three more types of *saalan* (gravy) for another twenty minutes on the phone, we finally bid goodbye. It was going to be a challenge. I had never before ordered such an extensive menu from a restaurant.

After pondering for a while, I picked up the piece of paper on which I had scribbled the items Sahab wanted for dinner.

I smiled as I thought of one person who would be able to help me with this seemingly insurmountable task. He was an old friend. His father owned a famous restaurant chain in Mumbai.

When he answered my call, I greeted him with the genuine warmth and respect I had towards him. I then proceeded to ask him if he would humour my request. Thankfully, he obliged. I proceeded to tell him the items we needed and all the necessary details Sahab had mentioned.

I informed him that although it was a food order, it would be like a catering job, but only for about eight to ten people. I knew that this was a test Dilip Sahab had laid out for me. He was probably testing my skills, checking my ability to overcome hurdles. I didn't want to fail.

"Please make sure that the order is perfect."

"Don't you worry, Faisal. I will make sure the food is delicious. Everything will be perfect."

"I need to ask for one more additional favour."

"Please, by all means."

"You will have to send two skilled people to serve the guests, preferably two of your best senior people. The cutlery will be provided by the hotel, so no need to carry that. Your people can coordinate with the hotel staff and make sure they have it ready by the time food is served."

"Is it a special guest of yours?"

"Yes. All of this is for Dilip Kumar Sahab."

"What! I hope you are not joking with me."

I laughed a little, hearing him so shocked.

"No. I'm not joking at all."

"Faisal, don't worry. I'll be there in person to serve the food if required."

I knew this was a man who wouldn't let me down. His restaurant was known for its delicious food and great service. Knowing that this order was for Dilip Sahab, they would take utmost care in delivering the best they ever have.

"I do have one more request."

"When your staff is done with dinner, Dilip Sahab will insist on paying. Please instruct them to not take any money from him. I will pay you for the food and service right now. Please inform Sahab that the bill has been taken care of."

"Faisal, I won't charge you for this food. It will be my honour to serve Dilip Kumar. How can I ask you to pay for something like this?"

I was touched. Although Dilip Kumar was an actor of the yesteryears by this time, he was still revered across generations.

"No, my friend. I insist on paying. You are doing me a huge favour by arranging for the food and the catering."

When I came back from Bangalore, I went to meet Sahab. All he did was give me raving reviews about the food and the service that was provided. He had loved every item. Weeks later, he still remembered the dinner and would tell me about it.

"Your friend got us some very delicious food that day."

Sahab asked me if I had paid the bill. I lied. I didn't want him to pay, so I assured him that I had taken the money from Saira baji instead.

It is probably the best money I have ever spent in my life.

Sahab would often try to humour us or pull our legs talking about food. He once asked me the English word for *heeng*.

"What do you call heeng in English?"

"Sahab, it's called asafoetida."

"What? Are you sure? That sounds like a strange word."

"Yes, Sahab. I'm sure. It's asafoetida."

I couldn't get enough. I loved being his very own Google. It was our 'thing' and I cherished it. Whenever he called, and whatever question he asked, I would make sure I had an answer for him, even if I was busy with something else.

Dilip Sahab was always conscious about the food he ate. He made sure that it was nutritious. All his life, he had taken good care of his health and it showed. Sahab indulged in junk food in moderation, that too only on special occasions. His diet consisted of eggs, healthy home-cooked meals and light snacks. Even when I visited him and the help would lay out delicious snacks for the guests, Sahab would stick to the healthy options. He was always open to trying new and different kinds of meals without going overboard.

I learnt from Dilip Sahab that whatever your age, gender, or size, it is important to eat a nourishing meal. Every bite you take should be for your health. It should contribute to your physical, mental as well as emotional well-being. This does not in any way mean that you stop eating. He used to believe that we should eat whatever our heart may desire, but also control our portions and sweat it out later.

I remember an evening in the early years of the millennium. The Olive Bar and Kitchen in Bandra was a popular place to hang out. Anyone who knows about Olive knows that it is *the* place to spot celebrities. Two of my friends and I decided to have dinner there. It was the ideal place for a quiet meal and had a good ambience. With its cane chairs, wooden tables and pebbles covering the floor, Olive had a relaxed vibe. The cuisine at Olive is European, Mediterranean and Italian (or so it was then). One of my friends was slightly disappointed with the menu.

"Why did we choose this place if we weren't going to enjoy the food."

My second friend chirped in, "Ambience, my dear friend."

I laughed at my friend's disappointment. "You are right though. I do prefer Indian food over American or European."

"But the ambience. What about the calm and peace? It's like you're at the beach, but with pebbles."

We both laughed. He was clearly in love with this place.

The conversation led to us discussing the idea of opening our own restaurant – how it would be located at Pali Hill, have a similar ambience, but serve real Indian food.

My friend, who was in love with the ambience, couldn't get enough of the idea.

My business mind wondered if we would ever make a profit from the proposed food joint, despite our discussion clearly being a mere means to pass the time.

"Do you think people will pay such exorbitant prices for Indian food?"

"It's fine dining, Faisal. People's mindset is evolving and they are more and more willing to pay for good food."

"What kind of Indian food would our restaurant serve, though? Indian cuisine is so vast."

"All kinds. We will put options from every state, every part of the country. We'll serve South Indian idlis, Awadhi Biryani, Hyderabadi *haleem*, Malayali prawns, Punjabi *kadhhi*, Bengali fish and every other Indian dish we can think of. It could be our own 'Mini India'."

I was intrigued and impressed. Were we really going to pull off such an extensive menu? The main course section would probably resemble a novel.

While we were busy discussing the new restaurant, its ambience and the menu, I realized that there was one man who knew more about food than I probably ever will. Dilip Sahab was a connoisseur who had travelled the globe extensively, interacted with scores of people from all parts of the world, loved to cook and most certainly loved to try new cuisines. He would have a few ideas that could help. On a whim, I called him.

Very few people know that for a brief period, Sahab had a mobile phone. The handset was a good old Nokia 5110, which Sahab usually left in the car and hardly ever answered. I think

Saira baji wanted him to use a mobile phone so he could be reached easily but he was not bothered about it. One day, when I had called him, his niece, who was visiting from the US, answered. When I had asked her where Dilip Sahab was, she told me that he had given her his phone as she was in need of a local number.

That day, however, when I called him on his mobile, I was able to get through to him. His driver Kutti answered the call.

"Hello."

"Hello, Kutti. Where are you? Is Sahab with you?"

"Yes, he is. Sir, we are returning home from Juhu. We're in the car."

"Kutti, can you pass the phone to Sahab?"

I heard a brief shuffle and then Dilip Sahab's voice on the other end.

"Sahab, are you going anywhere?"

Without answering my question, he asked me if I needed anything.

It was strange how the same man who spent hours talking on a landline was so impatient on a mobile phone. On the mobile phone, he kept it brief and to the point, using only monosyllabic replies. So, before he decided to hang up, I talked as fast and tersely as I could.

"I'm here at a restaurant with two of my friends. Your name came up, so I thought of asking if you would like to join us for dinner."

"Where are you now?"

"We're sitting at Olive in Pali Hill."

"Where exactly is that on Pali Hill?"

"Sahab, pass the phone to Kutti. I will explain it to him."

There was a brief shuffle again and then Kutti was back on the phone.

"Kutti, do you know the Olive restaurant at Pali Hill?"

"Yes, sir."

"Ok then, please bring Sahab there. How long will you take to reach?"

"Only ten minutes."

He hung up and I turned to my friends.

"Hey guys, Dilip Kumar will be joining us for dinner in the next ten minutes."

My friends looked at me like I was crazy. I was grinning at them. I couldn't believe my luck. I had seen Dilip Sahab ignore all incoming calls on his mobile phone, but this evening, I was able to reach him on it. I was thrilled.

My friends were in another zone. They could not believe that Dilip Kumar would be joining us for a meal. They thought that even if Sahab had said yes to dinner with us, he wasn't really going to turn up. They poked fun at me and I laughed along with them.

But soon, they had to stop laughing. Sure enough, at the entrance, we spotted Dilip Sahab entering the restaurant.

As soon as Dilip Sahab entered, all eyes turned towards him. Some smiled at him, some gently acknowledged him with polite nods, and some walked up to him for a photograph or an autograph. Dilip Sahab, being the gentleman, obliged everyone. Eventually, Sahab turned towards us. We had walked up to him in the meantime to escort him to our table.

Sahab walked with us to our table. Both my friends were quiet. They were too overwhelmed to even speak. Sahab, aware of their shock and in an attempt to make them feel at ease, started the conversation.

"So, tell me, what were you guys discussing?"

Realizing that they probably needed a slightly tougher nudge, I answered.

"We were thinking of starting a restaurant."

Sahab smiled. He looked at me like he was impressed with the idea we had so randomly come up with. One of my friends came out of his shock and started adding to the conversation. A lover of Indian cuisine, Sahab's face lit up as my friend spoke about the ideas he had.

"Sahab, we want to serve Indian food at the restaurant."

"What kind of Indian food?"

I chimed in. "All kinds. Veg, non-veg, North Indian, South Indian."

"That is a wonderful idea. You must keep another item on the menu."

My other friend finally spoke up. "Which item, Sahab?"

"Dilip Kumar kebab. And I will share the recipe with you."

We all burst out laughing. It was an exceptional idea and soon we were coming up with similar-sounding dishes. Eventually, we ordered dinner. Sahab insisted that he would have whatever we suggested. Happy, and humbled, I ordered soup and seafood for all of us. It was an evening well spent.

Our restaurant idea never bore fruit and we went back to our businesses. My friends, even today, fondly remember the dinner we had. They don't remember the food, but the conversation lives on in their minds. After they'd gone home, they told all their friends and family about the epic dinner they'd had with Dilip Sahab.

Word spread like wildfire and soon I was receiving numerous calls from their family and friends, requesting a few minutes with Dilip Sahab. I was overwhelmed. I couldn't believe how many people wanted to meet with him.

I immediately called up my friends. I wanted to yell at them for spreading the news, but instead we ended up reminiscing about the evening and laughed about how lucky we had been. I don't know why Sahab agreed to come that day, but I'm thankful he did.

18

A Man and His Faith

Dilip Sahab was a devout Muslim who respected all religions. Being a voracious reader, he had read several holy books and even memorized the Quran. His copy of the Quran had myriad scribblings along the margins, which were his thoughts on the commentary and understanding of certain sections of the holy book.

In Islam, the core article of faith is the belief that there is only one God, Allah, and that Muhammad is his messenger. A lot has been written about the faith, a lot has been speculated about the faith, but there is only one truth: Islam is a religion of peace. It is rooted in the values of humanity, kindness, strength, courage and honesty.

Prayers in Islam are known as *salah*, or namaz. A Muslim is required to pray to the Lord five times a day. The five prayers that one has to offer are *fajr*, the morning prayer; *dhuhr*, the early afternoon prayer; *asr*, the late afternoon prayer; *maghrib*, the sunset prayer; and *isha*, the night prayer.

I have prayed along with Sahab many times during the years I knew him. I would meet with him after work, and together, we would pray either on his terrace or on the lawns of 34/B Pali Hill. The entire household, including the help, used to offer prayers together. On one long mat, all the men would stand and bow (pray) in a straight line. On a mat behind the first one, Saira baji would be joined in prayers by the women of the household. One small mat would sit right in front for the imam, the one who leads the prayers.

Anyone from a group can be the imam. He need not be a religious scholar. Any Muslim in a state of *wudhu* (purity of body and thoughts), knows verses from the Quran and can recite them can be an imam.

Sahab, however, had appointed a religious scholar as the imam to lead the prayers at his house for the asr, maghrib and isha namaz.

Whatever Dilip Sahab's schedule was, he was particular about the asr and the maghrib prayers. I would usually join Sahab for the maghrib namaz. I have often watched and observed Sahab after these prayers. Even when the namaz was over, Dilip Sahab didn't get up. He would lift his hands, shut his eyes and pray to his Lord. He would talk to Allah. He would stay on the prayer mat for an extra ten to fifteen minutes.

I remember his eyes would fill with tears and his lips would move without any sound. I never asked him what he prayed for in those extra few minutes. The duas were silent. Perhaps he was thanking Allah for his countless mercies on him, throughout his life, perhaps he was asking the Lord to bless his dear mother and father and all his ancestors with the best of *jannat* (heaven). Was he going back in time and recalling the days of his childhood with his siblings and seeking forgiveness for himself and on their behalf? Perhaps he was worried about Saira baji's loneliness after he was gone, and seeking Allah's mercy on the household. Perhaps he was seeking Allah's blessings on his country and the land and the people who had showered him with so much love and affection throughout his life. Perhaps he was praying for his good health. Who knows what he was asking for in those duas? What Sahab prayed for was between him and his creator. But he was often teary-eyed during his duas.

On a few occasions, when Sahab took longer than usual to finish his prayers, I wouldn't stay back. If I had to attend an event, or if I had to rush back to the office, I used to excuse myself politely after informing Saira baji. Out of respect, I could never bring myself to tell Sahab that I had to take his leave.

I received a call from Sahab's assistant on one such occasion when I had left after maghrib. He called me up and said that Sahab had been looking for me. I remember my hands had started to sweat at the thought of Dilip Sahab looking for me after his prayers while I was absconding. I didn't want him to think I was being disrespectful. I had hoped that Sahab would not notice my absence while there were so many others around him, but then I realized that I was like family.

Sahab told me that he had noticed me sneak out after the prayers. Speaking to his assistant over the phone was one thing, but having this conversation in person was difficult. I was embarrassed.

"I sincerely apologize for leaving without meeting you," is all I could come up with.

Sahab held my hand and smiled. I think he was just trying to bring to my attention that he had noticed it. I felt a sense of relief as if there was somebody protecting me, like a father.

In health and in sickness, he always said that Allah was his companion. In December 2012, Sahab faced serious health concerns. His sugar levels had shot up and his creatinine levels were on the rise. Sahab was due to celebrate his ninetieth birthday but no one was in any mood for celebrations. Sahab indicated that he wanted to visit the house of his Lord, the Kaaba in Mecca. That is when Saira baji, and her brother, Sultan Ahmed, decided to act on his wishes. I received a last-minute phone call from Saira baji.

"Dilip Sahab wants us all to go together for umrah."

"Saira baji, I will be honoured. When do we leave?"

"We will leave in a few days. I am sending my assistant to your office. Please give him your passport and a few passport-size pictures. Zaka bhai of Fourways Travel will make all the required arrangements."

"I would love to perform umrah with all of you. I am very excited. This is going to be my first journey to Mecca."

Unfortunately, neither my wife, nor my children were able to come along. I wanted them to join us for the spiritual journey, but our children had school, so my wife chose to stay back. I cannot wait to take them to Mecca someday.

In Islam, an able-bodied and financially capable adult is required to do the hajj at least once in their lifetime. It is an annual pilgrimage, and Muslims from across the world gather at Mecca and Medina to pray to the almighty Allah during this time. It is a pilgrimage to the Kaaba. Located inside the courtyard of the Sacred Mosque of Mecca, it is known as the 'House of God'. It is the large black cubical structure many of you must have seen in photographs. While hajj is a once-a-year event, umrah is a smaller pilgrimage and can be performed any time of the year.

The umrah trip was planned for January 2013. By the time the dates were finalized, we had become an entourage of twenty-one people. In the large group, along with Dilip Sahab and Saira baji, were Sultan bhai and his family, Sahab's physician, Dr Arshad Ali, several household help, Asif bhai and I.

On 2 January, on a nippy winter day, we were packed and ready to leave. All the media houses knew that Dilip Kumar was travelling for the holy pilgrimage of umrah. Almost every newspaper was aware and the media in Mecca and Medina were looking forward to welcoming Dilip Sahab.

Due to his poor health and the last-minute commotion of travel, Sahab was slightly agitated. The attention around Sahab's trip meant that many photojournalists and reporters were parked outside Dilip Sahab's home on the day of the trip, ready to interview him and wish him well for his journey. This added to Sahab's agitation.

Saira baji, having been by her husband's side for more than half a century, could sense and understand his needs. She realized that the commotion and noise were causing him discomfort, but she also knew that Asif bhai's presence next to Sahab in the car would help him remain calm.

Before we left for umrah, I wanted the world to know Dilip Sahab's thoughts on his travel. I typed out a couple of lines on Sahab's Twitter and showed it to Saira baji and Sahab. Once they approved it, I sent out the tweet for the world to see.

I have already written about Sahab's initiation into Twitter-verse. By January 2013, Sahab had amassed a huge following. His followers were from a variety of age groups and generations. When I tweeted about Dilip Sahab's umrah from his account, the blessings and the good wishes had poured in. By the time we reached the airport, hundreds of people were already present there to wish him luck for the journey.

Due to Sahab's age at the time, he was unable to walk long distances. He required a wheelchair to navigate Mumbai's vast international airport. The enormous crowd gathered outside the airport created an unwanted hindrance to all of us. We had to fight our way to get inside the airport. Luckily, the Mumbai airport and CISF staff were there to assist us.

The journey for the holy pilgrimage of hajj begins at Mecca. After performing tawaf around the Kaaba and offering prayers, pilgrims head to Medina to visit the Masjid an-Nabwi, which is the Prophet's mosque. Historical records and folklore confirm that the Prophet Muhammad worked on the construction of this mosque. His resting place is within the mosque.

Since there is an international airport at Medina and the holy pilgrimage of umrah is not restricted by the rules of hajj, our travel company suggested that we visit Medina first. Zakaullah Siddiqui, chairman of Fourways Travel, one of India's leading hajj and umrah tour companies, personally accompanied us on the umrah. He ensured that we did not face any difficulty during our travel and stay in the holy cities.

Although we landed in Medina in the middle of the night, Dilip Sahab's fans were waiting for him at the airport. People walked up to him, requesting for pictures and autographs. Siddiqui had ensured that our immigration was done expeditiously by the kind and most welcoming Saudi Arabian authorities. Our only concern was to make sure Sahab reached the hotel comfortably. He was already agitated with the attention and we could sense that he was craving a little peace and some much-needed sleep after enduring the long travel from Mumbai.

As soon as we exited the airport, our rides were waiting to take us to the Oberoi Hotel. Thankfully, the hotel is situated right next to the mosque, so Sahab did not have to exert himself too much.

All of us retired to our rooms as soon as we reached the hotel. After a few hours of sleep, we woke up to the call for fajr prayers at the Masjid an-Nabwi. Considered one of the largest and oldest mosques in the world, it has a core part, where the imam leads thousands of people in prayer during salah. Behind that is a tomb-like structure that houses the grave of the Prophet Muhammad (SAW). Due to the never-ending crowd, only a lucky few manage to catch a glimpse of the Prophet's tomb, that too for a mere ten to twenty seconds.

During the dhuhr prayers, Sahab refused the wheelchair and chose to walk instead. Holding our hands, Sahab led the entire entourage.

As soon as we neared the tomb, almost every person standing around us dispersed. They saw Dilip Kumar in the mosque and made space for him to stand beside the tomb of the Prophet and offer his prayers. Dilip Sahab was visibly surprised.

The young Saudi security guards at the mosque were unable to understand why people would make way for an old man and why countless people surrounded him. Despite being unaware of who Dilip Kumar was, they didn't interfere or question us or the people around us and let us continue with our prayers. We decided to make the most of what we had, and offered a few *Nafl rakaats* (non-obligatory prayers) by the prophet's tomb.

After offering our prayers, we waited for the imam to begin the dhuhr prayer.

We left soon after the prayer was over. While leaving the mosque, people gathered around Sahab again. Outside the mosque, Sahab was now approachable to the scores of people around him. Despite being agitated, Sahab smiled and greeted whoever approached him. He was unable to remain calm for long though and was visibly upset at those who were clicking his pictures. Tired and hungry, Sahab wanted to return to the hotel as soon as possible.

We stayed in Medina for four days. On the fifth day, we departed for Mecca to carry out the compulsory rituals of umrah. At Mecca, we stayed at the Hilton Towers Hotel, where we were given excellent service and assistance. As soon as we checked into our rooms, we left for the grand mosque called Masjid Al-Haram, or the Sacred Mosque of Mecca.

In the centre of the mosque's courtyard lies the Kaaba. Being the most sacred site in Islam, Muslims consider the Kaaba to be *Bayt'Allah* or the House of God. When praying in any part of the world, a Muslim must always face in the direction of the Kaaba.

One of the core rituals during pilgrimage in Mecca is to go around the Kaaba seven times. The worshippers circle the Kaaba in a constant wave, humming prayers at all times. While performing the rounds one must be reciting prayers, proclaiming complete surrender to the Lord. This entire process is called tawaf. Sahab sat on the wheelchair as we started the tawaf. We stuck close to the Kaaba while making the rounds to ensure that we could make the rounds in a shorter period of time, considering Sahab was with us. If you've ever witnessed tawaf, you'd know that if even one person stops while making the rounds, it disrupts the entire flow and causes quite a commotion.

Unfortunately for us, whenever anyone noticed and recognized Dilip Sahab, they would stop and meet him. People clicked pictures of him, many stopped to shake his hands and dozens gathered around to meet him. One Turkish lady even stopped and kissed his hands during the tawaf. We wondered how uneasy Sahab might have felt. I had to ask people to back off. "We have come here to perform the tawaf. Please focus on yours too. This is the house of Allah."

While I was saying this, an old Afghan man came up to me. He had fair skin, light eyes and dark hair. His beard covered almost half his face and hung low till his chest. When he spoke, his words carried a heavy Afghan accent. He spoke to me in Urdu.

"Son, don't stop anyone from meeting Dilip Kumar. Who knows, maybe their wish is being granted today? In Allah's house, who are you to stop anyone?"

He turned around and disappeared into the crowd. I was stunned. What he had said made sense. Generations of people knew, admired and loved Dilip Sahab. That day, countless people didn't just have the opportunity to see him, but to pray next to him. They would have prayed for years to see one glimpse of him.

Truly, who was I to stop anyone? I was in God's house, and I was a mere man. A human who had no control over anyone or anything. I bowed in humility. I had learned another great lesson in the shadow of Dilip Sahab and I was lucky enough to have learnt it while performing the tawaf. I prayed for the Afghan man and thanked him for the deep insight he had provided me with.

In the following days, to make Sahab's pilgrimage easier, we decided that instead of asking people to stop approaching Sahab, all of us would surround him to obscure him from public view. It would allow him to pray in peace and cause minimal disturbance to other worshippers performing their rituals.

Our strategy worked, because the next day, with no one disturbing his commune with the Almighty, Sahab started reciting his prayers out loud. He seemed more energetic and there was a certain joy and peace in his voice. He seemed closer to God. There was a peculiar strength in his voice that I hadn't heard in a long time. His enthusiasm was infectious. As he recited the Arabic prayers out loud, we followed him.

After our umrah was complete, we visited the various historical sites in and around Mecca the next day. We fell in love with the city and decided to extend our trip by a few more days. It was Allah's mercy that Siddiqui was with us, so the modifications in travel plans were not a hassle. He took care of them. During this time, a lot of Saudi newspapers tried to get in touch with us to interview Sahab. Upon Sahab's request, I spoke on his behalf, narrating the spiritual journey we'd had. Sahab also met a few dignitaries who called on him at the hotel, before we finally departed.

There was a drastic improvement in Sahab's mood, health and overall well-being after the trip. He was more joyous and his outlook seemed brighter.

At the Mumbai airport, as expected, we were received by a lot of reporters and fans. Saira baji spoke a few words to express her gratitude for being able to complete the umrah with such ease. My wife had also come to the airport to receive us. My spirits were high after the umrah journey and my family could sense it.

As I reflected on our journey, I realized how lucky we were. We had performed umrah without any difficulties. At the age of ninety years, Allah granted Dilip Sahab the energy to carry out the umrah and that is more than what we could have asked for. We hadn't thought Sahab would be able to complete the entire umrah, but we were proved wrong. In fact, on many occasions during the umrah, Sahab had decided to leave the wheelchair and walk.

The journey of umrah is a spiritual and uplifting one. For me, personally, it was even more so. It was my first international trip with Sahab and what a trip it was. I could not have asked for a better journey. I thank the Lord that he gave me this once-in-a-lifetime opportunity.

I have never had any detailed discussion with Sahab about faith and religion. But based on his chats with me, I have learnt that Sahab's outlook has always been all-encompassing and non-rigid. He loved and believed in his religion, but he was not one to impose it on others. He never judged others over their faith, or lack thereof, or preach about his own. He believed that each person had their own beliefs. Some aligned with his, some didn't, and that was all right.

He had true respect for other religions in a manner that he has even embodied them for roles in his movies. In *Gunga Jumna*, he played a devout Hindu with such conviction that some fans, even today, are unable to believe that Dilip Kumar is in fact a Muslim. Yusuf Khan is a Muslim, but Dilip Kumar wasn't bound by a religious identity.

A few times, I accompanied him when he was invited to mosques and gatherings, often when a well-known scholar, or maulana, would visit. Every time, the crowd gathered would be in thousands. Sometimes I wondered if they were there for the maulana or to meet Dilip Sahab, or both.

A few years ago, Abrarul Haq, a renowned maulana, visited Bandra's famous Jama Masjid, situated on the busy Swami Vivekananda Road. Many leading maulanas and imams wanted to meet Dilip Sahab when they visited Mumbai. Whenever his schedule permitted, Sahab would meet them at home.

Maulana Abrarul Haq's representative had indicated his willingness to come and see Sahab. Dilip Sahab, though, insisted that he would come to Jama Masjid instead. Both the men were of the same age, so comfort and convenience were what Sahab had in mind for the maulana.

Sahab had asked me to accompany him. We reached well before the maghri has circles of people around it in concentric form. Like a constant wave, it is humming with people and their prayers at all times.

Dilip Sahab met the maulana, and we all stood together as the maulana led the prayer. After the prayer, the maulana is required to sit on a chair, facing the audience. The maulana insisted that Sahab sat first, and sahab insisted that the maulana be seated first. It gave way to the age-old debate of *pehle aap* (you first), and ended with Sahab and the maulana holding hands and sitting down together.

That day I realized that no matter how successful you become, it is important to never forget your roots. Be it your faith, your family, your friends, your well-wishers, don't ever forget anybody who loves you, or take them for granted.

*

Sahab's magnanimity, humility and hard work were recognized when he was awarded the Padma Vibushan, India's second-highest civilian award in India. In 2015, Sahab's health had further deteriorated and travel was a cause for concern. To accommodate his special circumstances and breaking established protocols, the president and the honourable prime minister of India requested the Union home minister to personally visit Sahab's home and bestow the award upon him. As the shawl was wrapped around him and he was presented with the citation and medal, Saira Banu, his proud and loving wife, stood beside him and bowed on his behalf. I can say without any hesitation that Dilip Sahab did the award proud. It is mystifying that he was not bestowed the Bharat Ratna.

Sahab never let Yusuf Khan become bigger than Dilip Kumar. He always maintained his dignity and humility. As he said memorably, *"Log aate hain mujhse Dilip Kumar ki batein karte hain. Dilip Kumar ka zikr hota hai. Mujhe lagta hai woh koi aur hai."* (People come and talk to me about Dilip Kumar. Dilip Kumar is discussed. I feel like he is someone else.)